INTERACTIVE AND DIGITAL MEDIA FOR EDUCATION IN VIRTUAL LEARNING ENVIRONMENTS

Interactive and Digital Media for Education in Virtual Learning Environments

Cai Yiyu
Editor

Nova Science Publishers, Inc.
New York

Additional color graphics may be available in the e-book version of this book.

LIBRARY OF CONGRESS CATALOGING-IN-PUBLICATION DATA
Yiyu, Cai.
Interactive and digital media for education in virtual learning
environments / Cai Yiyu.
p. cm.
Includes index.
ISBN 978-1-61668-844-8 (hardcover)
1. Computer-assisted instruction. 2. Interactive multimedia. 3. Distance
education. 4. Shared virtual environments. I. Title.
LB1028.5.Y59 2009
371.33'468--dc22
2010025526

Published by Nova Science Publishers, Inc. † New York

CONTENTS

PREFACE

Education has a complex nature. The rapid globalization has called for a profound change in educational methodology, and innovative use of new educational technology. Grounded in sound pedagogy, supported by solid research methodology, and with inter-/multi-discipline background, this book provides an integrated view on this paradigm shift for education. The book presents several educational projects developed or currently under development in different countries including Denmark, The Netherlands, Sweden, UK and Singapore. The emphasis of the book is placed on the research of innovative tools and approaches, and development of new learning environments to create new knowledge that could potentially transform teaching and learning. A special interest of the book is Interactive & Digital Media (IDM) technologies that leverage interactivity and immersive visualization, foster students' critical and creative thinking, and engage students in deeper and wider learning. From a more general sense, IDM in this book refers to an interdisciplinary field covering Game, Animation, Virtual Reality, Simulation, Computer Graphics, Visualization, Human-computer Interaction, Online Virtual Community, and so on.

Educators, researchers and developers work together in this book to exchange their ideas on pedagogy, enabling technology and their learning applications. In Chapter 1, Yam San Chee from the National Institute of Education (Singapore) looks into game-based learning from the perspective of pedagogy and epistemology. In Chapter 2, Elisabet M. Nilsson and Gunilla Svingby from the School of Education with Malmö University shared their Swedish experience on Simulation and Game for Science Classrooms. In Chapter 3, Thomas Duus Henriksen from the Danish School of Education with the University of Aarhus (Denmark) investigates the issues of fun, content and realism with learning games. In Chapter 4, Karin Tweddell Levinsen from the Institute of Curriculum Studies with Danish School of Education – Aarhus University discusses the implementation of Learning Management System (LMS) in Danish educational organizations. In Chapter 5, Sara de Freitas and Ian Dunwell from the Serious Game Institute with the University of Coventry (UK) explore the implications of interactivity, immersion and fidelity on the development of serious games with Second Life as a platform. In Chapter 6, Arthur van Bilsen from Delft University of Technology (The Netherlands) describes the potential of 3D visibility analysis in Virtual Learning Environments and Interactive & Digital Media. In Chapter 7, Norman Kiak Nam Kee and Noel Kok Hwee Chia from Early Childhood and Special Needs Education with the National Institute of Education (Singapore) focuses on the discussion of mediated and engaged learning in special education for children with autism spectrum disorders using commercial-off-the-shelf video games. In Chapter 8, Ban Hoe Chow and Kah Lay So from River Valley

High School (Singapore) share their experience using Virtual Reality technology for classroom teaching and student-based project work. In Chapter 9, Gwee Hwee Ngee from Hwa Chong Institution (Singapore) presents her initial trial with her secondary school students on the novel use of Virtual Reality technology for the application in Geometry Learning.

Associate Professor Yiyu CAI, Ph D
Nanyang Technological University
Republic of Singapore

In: Interactive and Digital Media for Education in Virtual … ISBN: 978-1-61668-844-8
Editor: Cai Yiyu

Chapter 1

POSSESSION, PROFESSION, AND PERFORMANCE: EPISTEMOLOGICAL CONSIDERATIONS FOR EFFECTIVE GAME-BASED LEARNING

Yam San Chee
National Institute of Education
Nanyang Technological University, Singapore

ABSTRACT

Educational games have been widely available since the advent of multimedia technology. Current state-of-the-art games, however, offer users 3D immersion and a depth of engagement that far exceed what was possible with multimedia. Unfortunately, the design of 3D games for education and learning has continued to lack both power and effectiveness due to a weak understanding, amongst game designers, of pedagogical and epistemological factors that are vital for designing effective game-based learning. In this chapter, I critically examine several commonly available online educational games. I argue that the weaknesses of game design stem centrally from an inadequate understanding of epistemology. I then explicate the needed epistemological understanding for effective game-based learning in terms of: (1) the fallacy of knowledge possession, (2) the inadequacy of knowledge profession, and (3) the necessity of knowing through performance. Next, I provide an example of game-based learning that illustrates how educational games can be taken to a new level of pedagogical and epistemological effectiveness. I conclude the chapter by considering some challenges to scaling up the adoption of game-based learning in schools.

KEYWORDS: game-based learning, epistemology, possession, profession, performance, *Legends of Alkhimia*, chemistry games

INTRODUCTION

Computer-based educational games have been available since the late 1980s when authoring tools such as Authorware™ and Macromedia Director™ (both now owned by Adobe Systems) became available. With the advent of Macromedia Flash™ (now also owned by Adobe Systems) in 1996, the initial trickle of educational games has grown into a sizeable flood, and computer-based games, purporting to have educational value, are now as commonplace as off-the-shelf products.

The Serious Game Initiative, launched in 2002 by the Woodrow Wilson International Center for Scholars, provided fresh impetus for the development of computer-based games that serve some kind of educational purpose rather than that of primarily entertaining the player. The term "serious game" was first coined by Abt (1970). It was used to refer to games and simulations that could be used to train decision makers in industry, government, and education, as well as in the field of personal relations. The targeted scope of application of such games is considerably wider today. The Wikipedia entry[1] for "serious game" states that the term refers to "products used by industries like defence, education, scientific exploration, health care, emergency management, city planning, engineering, religion, and politics." In a similar vein, Zyda (2005) defines a serious game as one that "uses entertainment to further government or corporate training, education, health, public policy, and strategic communication objectives." From the foregoing, it should be evident that education-centric games are only a subset of the larger serious games enterprise. Furthermore, the degree to which entertainment value is regarded as essential remains moot.[2]

In this chapter, I shall focus on computer games created for game-based learning. Such games are designed to achieve explicitly targeted learning outcomes. As part of my critical considerations, I shall consider what kinds of learning processes and outcomes are meaningful and desirable from an epistemological perspective.

In the sections that follow, I shall first critique several examples of educational games that are readily available or are upheld as good exemplars by established organizations in the serious games market. Next, I shall interrogate the underlying assumptions concerning the nature of knowledge that these games implicitly adopt. As part of this interrogation, I shall argue against (1) the fallacy of knowledge possession, and (2) the inadequacy of knowledge profession; then, I shall argue in favor of (3) the necessity of knowing through performance. Drawing upon my own research, I shall describe a game that illustrates how design for game-based learning can be enhanced through a deep understanding of epistemology and pedagogy. The conclusion of the chapter will consider some challenges to advancing game-based learning in an epistemologically informed way.

---

[1] http://en.wikipedia.org/wiki/Serious_games

[2] In saying this, I am not suggesting that educational games should not be fun to play. It is well known that playing computer games such as World of Warcraft involve substantial, sustained effort; hence, playing games can be "hard work." I would like to suggest instead that fun can arise from intrinsic satisfaction experienced through personally meaningful game play rather than predominantly from sensual pleasure.

Critique of Commonly Available Online Educational Games

Prensky's (2001) book on "Digital Game-based Learning" helped to popularize the use of computer games for learning. His idea of digital game-based learning is exemplified in the following quotation:

> "Most simply put, Digital Game-Based Learning is any marriage of *educational content* and computer games. The premise behind Digital Game-Based Learning is that it is possible to combine computer video games with a wide variety of *educational content*, achieving as good or better results as through traditional learning methods in the process." (pp. 145–146; italics added).

The emphasis on educational content that students are supposed to learn falls prey to Postman and Weingartner's (1969) critique of the notion that a classroom lesson is largely composed of two components, namely content and method. Content is always thought of as the "substance" of the lesson; it is something that students are supposed to "get." Such content exists independently of and prior to the student, and it is indifferent to the media by which it is "transmitted." Method constitutes the manner in which the content is presented; in this case, it is accomplished through the design embedded in the computer game. The framing implicit in this depiction of what digital game-based learning seeks to achieve is one of instructional design (Smith & Ragan, 1999) rather than learning design (Gagnon & Collay, 2006). In short, students learn the content they are taught, be it by a human teacher or by a computer game.

Let me now critically examine several examples of educational games that can be found on the Internet or for which information about these games can be readily found on the Internet. For the sake of convenience, I shall consider games in the domain of chemistry because this is one of the subject domains that I have been working in, as exemplified in the example of effective game-based learning later in this chapter.

I begin by considering an example from funbasedlearning.com. On accessing one of the links on the web page, one is presented with an instruction screen that states: "This is a fun little game that quizzes you on element names, symbols, and uses." Upon clicking the button "Start Element Quiz", one is presented with a question such as:

Hydrogen is

a. H
b. Yd
c. He
d. Hg

The onscreen hyperlink "How do I play this?" brings up the following instructions: "Click on the answer link for each question and a message will pop up letting you know if it's correct. If you miss one of the 43 questions, don't worry, it'll come up again until you get it right."

Critical readers will recognize that the questions posed on the web page are merely multiple-choice questions that form the staple diet of school assessments. It is quite remarkable that the quiz designers position this activity as a "fun little game" and even phrase the link to help information as "How do I *play* this?" (italics added). In addition, it should be evident that this model of learning with a "game" subscribes to the content and method model of teaching referred to by Postman and Weingartner. The "game designers" appear to believe that there is considerable learning value to be derived from knowing "elemental facts" such as "Hydrogen is H", "O is oxygen", etc.

Let me now consider a second example. It comes from sheppardsoftware.com. Selecting the "Chemistry Games" link, one is taken to a page with "Periodic Table Games". A typical example of such a game is one that shows the periodic table, with the following instruction: "Click on the element with the atomic mass of 58.693." If one selects the incorrect element in the periodic table, the system feedback is "Oops, that is incorrect. Please try again." A second incorrect attempt leads to the system flashing the correct element that needs to be selected. Selecting the flashing element then leads to the feedback "Correct!!!" accompanied by the presentation of extensive information about that element.

Would any student care to remember that nickel is the element that has an atomic mass of 58.693? What does the design of such a "game" suggest about the designer's conception of 'knowledge' and what is worth learning?

A White Paper on serious games that was written for Adobe Systems[3] contains many game examples that are presumably regarded as good exemplars. The section on "Games in schools" shows the following example.

What may a sponsor of the DiDA Olympics provide?

Correct!

Money would help the team with items like transport.

However: What else could they provide to support the team and perhaps promote themselves?

- Good weather
- Athletes
- Team kit
- Money

The author of the White Paper asserts: "Younger learners are also being exposed to serious games with great success. England's North West Learning Grid, for example, launched DiDA Delivered, a diploma program in IT skills for secondary students in the U.K. The curriculum includes 4,000 learning objects and 300 serious games" (p. 8).

Do serious games such as the ones illustrated above make a credible claim for educating children? Is the ability to answer content questions correctly helpful to preparing students for life in the 21st century?

Ascending the ladder of educational game sophistication, we encounter examples such as the one found at chemistryteaching.com. One particular instance focuses on atoms, symbols, and equations. Via an interface comprising both text and molecular representations, the student is tasked to "balance the equation for the combustion of methane." The left hand side of the window shows the "Reactants" methane and oxygen, while the right hand side shows the "Products" carbon dioxide and water. The student is instructed as follows: "Click on each

---

[3] Found at www.adobe.com/resources/elearning/pdfs/serious_games_wp.pdf

of the molecules in turn, until you have a balanced equation, then click OK." The correct answer, represented as a chemistry equation, is:

$$CH_4 + 2O_2 \rightarrow CO_2 + 2H_2O$$

That is, one molecule of methane and two molecules of oxygen react to form one molecule of carbon dioxide and two molecules of water. Given that the products are already stated in the body of the question, the equation balancing exercise becomes quite trivial. The student merely varies the number of each type of molecule in the chemistry equation.

Another type of chemistry "game" that can be found online is the virtual chemistry laboratory. An attractive instance of this "game" is available at virtlab.com. There is considerable sophistication in the design of the virtual laboratory and the kinds of experiments that students can perform. It appears that the designer's goal is to replace the highly constrained chemistry laboratory experiments that students typically perform in school with a digital version of the same. The instructions provided for performing the laboratory experiments are procedural. They require the student to execute a sequence of steps in strict order. However, this digital version of a chemistry laboratory is a simulation; it is not a game.

Prensky (2001, 2007) has articulated what he views as the differences between simulations and games. He states that a "pure simulation" focuses on the thing or process being simulated, while a "pure game" focuses on the user's experience. In particular, the purpose of a "pure simulation" is practice; it copies reality, is life-paced, assumes an externally defined meaning, and entails no goals, no story, and no struggle. "Pure games", by contrast, have entertainment as their purpose. They include elements of fantasy, are game-paced, require players to construct their own meaning, and involve a struggle to achieve meaningful goals within a flow of narrative. The game characteristics highlighted by Prensky are absent in VirtLab. Hence, VirtLab, while a useful learning tool, is a simulation and not a game. Its ultimate goal is to help train students' skills in typical school-based laboratory work.

Abstracting from the above examples, I draw the following inferences. First, readily available chemistry games overwhelmingly attempt to teach students chemistry content. The rationale underlying the game's design is that of "teaching content." The emphasis of such games is to drill student mastery of declarative propositions and to have students be able to state what is 'right' and what is 'wrong' (alternatively, what is 'true' and what is 'false'). Such subject content is seen as 'knowledge', an invaluable resource that teachers want students to acquire as part of the education enterprise. The second inference concerns the matter of skills. The predominant view of 'knowledge' is that it can be subdivided between declarative knowledge and procedural knowledge. Thus, apart from the knowledge-as-content focus, teachers and curriculum designers also concern themselves with the development of students' chemistry skills. To this end, the study of chemistry is accompanied by mandated laboratory sessions where students are required to execute a fixed set of sequential steps that adheres to a template of 'the right method' to perform the chemistry experiment. To perform any steps other than those included in 'the right method' would bring about penalties; there could also be dangerous outcomes. While the motivation that underlies wanting students to do the experiment 'right' is understandable, the side effect is that students never develop a deep understanding of why 'right' is (deemed to be) 'right'. In practice, 'right' can only be understood *in relation to* its opposite: namely, 'wrong'. 'Right', in isolation, can carry no meaning; 'right' can only come to mean in relation to everything else that is 'not right'. This idea is well established in the domains of semiotics (Thwaites, Davis, & Mules, 2002) and, more broadly, literary theory (Klages, 2006). While available chemistry laboratory simulation software usually permits students to commit errors, they are typically allowed to commit only inconsequential errors. Similar to intelligent tutoring systems in design, such simulations do not allow for open-ended experimentation because the developers very deliberately want students to learn only to 'do the right thing'. Taking steps that are 'not right' is viewed as not having any value for learning; it is a waste of time. Consequently, students' experience of chemistry phenomena is highly circumscribed to the subset of steps that relate to 'the right procedure' only.

To summarize, chemistry game designers, in general, make certain basic assumptions about what it means to 'learn chemistry'. First, they assume that one learns chemistry by *acquiring* 'the right answer' to factual questions. Second, they assume that chemistry laboratory sessions are intended primarily for students to experience and confirm prescribed standard experiments. Mastery of laboratory procedures is thus assessed in terms of students having *acquired* the target set of skills to execute those procedures. Are such assumptions tenable?

Epistemology for Game-Based Learning

In this section of the chapter, I wish to argue that computer games open up new pathways for learning, based on the unique aspects of learning in the first-person that the medium affords. As part of my critical interrogation of computer games as media for learning and my examination of implicit assumptions related to knowledge that are embedded in commonly available chemistry games above, I seek to make a case for a deeper understanding of epistemology in relation to game-based learning. In the section following, I then seek to illustrate the conceptual ideas with a positive example of design for game-based learning.

The Fallacy of Knowledge Possession

'Knowledge' is commonly thought of as something that a person 'has'. A recent article in the local newspaper proclaimed: "Trawling for knowledge." The article sought to highlight how easily students can 'obtain knowledge' from the Internet these days. All that students need do is 'let down their nets' on the Internet, and knowledge, like fish, will be caught. One may argue that the title merely plays on an analogy. However, analogies and metaphors powerfully reveal the underlying conceptualizations that people hold when they think and speak of various phenomena (Lakoff & Johnson, 1980).

We can trace the widespread belief that knowledge, like fish, is something that we possess to teachers who inculcate in their students, at a young age, that a dictionary contains the meanings of words. The dictionary software on my Macintosh computer, for example, provides the following definition of the word 'dog' (as a noun) among others: "a domesticated carnivorous mammal that typically has a long snout, an acute sense of smell, and a barking, howling, or whining voice. It is widely kept as a pet or for work or field sports." Students are led to believe that the meaning of the word 'dog' is *contained in* the definition and that being able to state or to recognize the definition constitutes 'having knowledge'. Thus, it is common enough to hear a classroom teacher say, "Go and find the meaning of [some word] in the dictionary." Over time, students imbibe a deep belief that memorizing propositional assertions such as the definition of the word 'dog' constitutes 'knowledge' that they 'possess'.

But what do we 'really' find in a dictionary? We find only carbon on paper, the "stuff" of which a dictionary is made (assuming that the dictionary has been produced by standard printing processes). No doubt, the carbon is laid out in very specific and stylized forms that constitute the basis of a natural language. However, it remains undeniable that, at the elemental material level, all that we have in a dictionary is carbon laid out on paper. Looking at different dictionaries will yield different definitions of the *same* word (even assuming that we choose the definition intended to convey the same *sense* of the word). This observation illustrates the claim that all we find and can ever hope to find in a dictionary is a *representation* of the dictionary author's *intended meaning*. It is not the meaning itself. Representations of meaning have no power to contain or bear meaning in and of themselves. As stated by Korzybski (1994), the map is not the territory. It is only a *representation* of the territory, and many different representations of the same territory are possible. Meaning arises instead through personal construction. It is an *interpretive* process that takes place within a social and cultural context, and it yields plausible interpretations of the author's (or the speaker's) communicative intent (Berger & Luckmann, 1966; Gergen, 1994).

The argument above is valid for *any* form of representation, including, but not limited to, images, sounds, and gestures. Hayakawa and Hayakawa (1990) explain how a symbol is not the thing symbolized. In semiotic terms, the signifier is not the thing signified. In both instances, the former term (symbol, signifier) relates to a verbal, intensional world, while the latter term (the thing symbolized, the thing signified) relates to the extensional world. The intensional and extensional are not identical. The intensional is used as a short-hand reference to denote the extensional. From an epistemological point of view, the conflation of the representation and the thing represented arises from a *dualist ontology* that assumes the existence of two distinct worlds: the 'out there' of the extensional world (we might refer to this as the 'reality' out there) and the 'in here' of the intensional world (we might refer to this as the 'reality' of our mental, in-me experience) (Gergen, 1999). This dualism is a side effect of the classical mind-body problem that assumes a *correspondence* between descriptions of the 'external' world and descriptions of the 'internal' mental world. However, as Gergen makes clear, no one-to-one correspondence is possible between what happens 'out there' and our descriptions of it 'in here'. To reinforce the point, try the following thought experiment. Take any five people who have just shared a common experience, and ask them to describe that experience individually. What will you get? You will obtain five different accounts, often very different from one another.

What then of the common view that human memory is the place where we 'store' our knowledge? If knowledge, unlike fish, is not a thing as I have argued, clearly it cannot be stored, whether in a memory data store or some other form of storage. The view of memory as a data store of some kind arises directly from the computer metaphor adopted by the psychology of human information processing. It is indeed noteworthy that early experimental work by Bartlett (1932) on what we would commonly call memory experiments today was framed in terms of the cognitive process of *remembering*. The idea associated with the term "memory" was not that memory is a store for mental objects but, rather, of memory as a *process*. Likewise, Rosenberg (1988) argues that memory, as it is widely conceived, is an invention: a piece of make-believe that has no credible basis in light of what is known from neuroanatomy and neurophysiology today. It is simply not credible to assert that brains have the ability to store symbolic and image representations qua symbolic and image representations (Damasio, 1994). Such an assertion gives rise to a fundamental type mismatch error. If one then accepts the argument that (1) knowledge is not a 'thing' and, furthermore, that (2) knowledge is not stored in memory because memory is a process of remembering rather than a knowledge store, it follows that humans cannot and do not possess knowledge *as commonly conceived*. To believe otherwise is to accept the fallacy of knowledge possession. Denying the fallacy of knowledge possession also implies that knowledge *cannot* be transmitted from one person to another. This understanding raises deep issues for the practice of teaching and learning in schools.

The Inadequacy of Knowledge Profession

The argument that knowledge is not a thing naturally begs the question, "What then is knowledge?" Allen Newell, in delivering his presidential address to the American Association for Artificial Intelligence in 1980, already echoed his own misgivings about the widespread conception of knowledge as a thing. He suggested instead that "knowledge is a competence-like notion, being a *potential* for generating action" (Newell, 1982, p.100, italics added). Recognizing that encoded knowledge representations of programmed behaviors (in the context of artificial intelligence) only create a potential to act intelligently, we might say that Newell conceived of knowledge as 'actionable knowledge'; that is, knowledge must be manifestable through *action*. We propose that a better term for 'actionable knowledge' is 'knowing' as this latter term more strongly connotes knowledge-in-action. When people act in a knowing way, they provide us with a basis to *impute* having knowledge. But to do so would entail accepting the fallacy of knowledge possession discussed above, something that I do not wish to do.

Based on the discussion above, it becomes important to distinguish between a person's ability to merely state or articulate ideas, that is, to profess 'knowledge', and that person's ability to act in ways that actualize the ideas in ways that are productive and useful both to him or herself as well as to others. In this sense, then, to profess knowledge is merely to articulate representations of knowledge. It is distinct from being able to *enact* what that 'knowledge' may entail in everyday life. An example that illustrates this point clearly is the case of swimming. The value of learning to swim lies in the act: the ability to swim so that one does not have to drown in water, etc. But the ability to swim is vastly different from the ability to deliver a lecture *about* swimming. The word 'about' signifies that one is operating in the realm of knowledge representation, not the realm of knowing as a capacity to act in the world. The difference in outcomes between swimming and lecturing about swimming and the relative value associated with each of those outcomes should be self-evident. On their own, verbal professions are cheap and plentiful. The uncomplimentary saying that "those who can, do; while those who can't, teach" illustrates the argument. However, making this assertion would only reflect on the speaker's own limited understanding of the challenges that educators face in facilitating student learning. They do not "merely teach". The mere (verbal and expository) profession of 'knowledge' is of very limited efficacy for genuine learning, as any student who has been on the receiving end of 'lectures' will attest to. In a similar vein, Minick (1987) has distinguished between communication *about* words and communication *with* words. The former is typical of communication within schooling while the latter marks a capacity to use words instrumentally in everyday actions. Thus, knowledge profession falls short of the enterprise of educating students. Being told does not automatically translate into the ability to enact or perform what one is told (Chee, 2002). Knowledge profession is thus inadequate.

The Necessity of Knowing Through Performance

The notion of performance derives from theatre studies (Schechner, 2003, 2006). In this domain, performance is always a form of enaction (Masciotra, Roth, & Morel, 2007). It involves a form of patterned behavior that entails repeated doing and re-doing. Consider a concert pianist who practises extensively for a recital. Practice on the piano clearly requires repeated playing and re-playing of the concert pieces. More important is the pianist's self-consciousness of the doing and re-doing. Such activity is both reflexive as well as reflective. The pianist is able to make himself the subject or focus of critical attention. With this reflexive perspective, the pianist experiences a "double consciousness": that is, there is a distinct awareness of that which is *actual* (how she actually played) and that which is *ideal* (how she actually wished to play). It is this tension between consciousness of an actual performance contrasted with that of an ideal performance that makes players aware of discrepancies between actual and ideal. The learning of the individual is propelled by awareness of the discrepancies between the actual performance and the ideal performance.

Enactive knowing, via performance, is inherently embodied in nature. A person engages in performance with his entire bodily being, or self. Learning, from this point of view, therefore entails transformations that relate to the entire self, not just the person's 'mind'. In this conception, it is the *person* that learns, not the 'mind' of the person. What, after all, is a mind? It is surely not an object that we possess. (Should the reader think otherwise, he is invited to locate where his mind resides.) Like 'knowledge', 'mind' is not an object that a person might have one (Chee, Tan, & Lee, 2010). An alternative framing is to understand a 'mind' as being imputed to persons who demonstrate the capacity of minding, as explained by Geertz (1973).

Following from the above, the site at which there is a tension between an actual performance and the ideal performance is a site for learning to take place. Indeed, it is this very tension between the actual and the ideal that drives learning forward. This site constitutes a border area where new negotiations of meaning and inventions of new practices can take place. Such border areas are the source of new ideas and new cultural practices.

Coming to know is therefore not a matter of mastering 'content' at all. Rather, it requires that learning take place in the context of inquiry into (some aspect of) life itself. This form of learning was clearly espoused by Dewey (Dewey, 1938/1991; Hickman, 1998). It is based on a conception of education as "the process of forming fundamental dispositions, intellectual and emotional, toward nature and fellow-man" (Garrison, 1998, p. 63). Fundamental to this conception is the paramount importance of the unity of "trans-action" between the learner, always a part of nature, and the rest of nature. In this mode of behavior, activity is the primary mode of learning. As explained by Garrison (1998, citing Dewey), the idea and the emotional excitation are constituted at one and the same time, and they represent the tension of stimulus and response within the coordination that makes up the mode of behavior. Explicit thinking arises a moment later, upon analysis and abstraction, as part of a process that discriminates between the organism (or learner) and the environment. Thus, coming to know does not arise from 'justified true belief', an assertion of classical epistemology, where logical forms are *imposed* on the subject matter of inquiry. Instead, the epistemology advocated here is a *performance epistemology*, one that views and values knowing as an ability to perform in ways that create personal, social, economic, and creative value. In this sense, therefore, we argue in favor of the necessity of knowing through performance, a pragmatic stance that is consonant with Dewey's philosophy.

GAME-BASED LEARNING GROUNDED ON PERFORMANCE EPISTEMOLOGY

We have been developing a game for chemistry education at the lower secondary school level in Singapore. The game, *Legends of Alkhimia*, instantiates a learning environment for students to learn chemistry by *doing* chemistry as part of a process of learning by inquiry (Dewey, 1938/1991; Postman & Weingartner, 1969), rather than learning *about* chemistry in order to "acquire chemistry knowledge." The game comprises eight levels of game play. It is a multi-player game that supports up to four students in each game session. Students learn chemistry within a framework of game-based learning called the Play–Dialog–Performance (PDP) Model (Chee, in preparation). This model of learning is technology mediated, through the artifact of the computer game, as well as socially mediated, through a dialogic mode of learning (Bakhtin, 1981; Wells, 1999) that takes place in a teacher-facilitated classroom context.

The game begins in Level 1 with a scenario where the four players crash-land in the environs of the ancient town of Alkhimia. They have with them certain weapons, a form of gun, that shoot ammunition drawn from cartridges attached to the weapons. On exiting their aircraft and surveying the surroundings, several monsters, emerging from a narrow mountain passageway, suddenly attack them. The players use their weapons against the monsters. (See Figure 1.[4]) However, they find that their weapons often jam, and their ammunition is of limited effectiveness against the monsters. After a short and furious battle, the monsters retreat back into the mountains. The players wonder why their weapons were prone to jamming. They also wonder about the composition of their ammunition and why it failed to kill the monsters.

The game narrative above sets the context for student engagement in a process of inquiry. Prior to entering into the game world, the players are positioned by the game as aspiring scientists (chemists) who learn their craft under the tutelage of their boss, Master Aurus. In the game lobby, they choose their in-game name. They also select their personal look in the player customization screen in a manner that reflects their sense of personal identity at the commencement of the game. Figure 2 illustrates the different attributes that a player can

[4] Note that the user interface elements are incomplete at this time because the game is still in development at the time of writing.

customize to represent herself through. As game play proceeds, the game narrative as well as the game interface provide opportunities for the player to modify the avatar's look and feel so as to foreground the values they adhere to via their self-presentation. In a later game level, players have to choose a piece of armour for themselves. The armour choices are designed so as to represent different kinds of symbols such as those representing notations related to chemistry or signs that depict an accomplished warrior. By observing the symbols or signs that students choose, we are able to make certain inferences about the kind of identity any individual student wishes to project. From a research point of view, these observations will be further complemented by data drawn from student interviews in order that a more richly textured understanding of a student's performative identity can be constructed.

Figure 1. Players warding off the monster attack in Level 1 of the game.

As the game proceeds, Master Aurus communicates with the players via an in-game communication device and asks them to return to their headquarters. Here, Master Aurus directs them to try purifying their ammunition substance. He has a suspicion that the substance has been contaminated, leading it to be ineffective against the monsters they previously encountered and causing their weapons to jam. This game narrative establishes the context for the players to be individually teleported to their personal chemistry laboratory bench where, as individuals, they seek to apply separation techniques to the ammunition substance to derive pure substances that can be used afresh against the monsters. Figure 3 illustrates what it is like to work at the in-game laboratory bench. In this illustration, the player attempts to separate two substances using a separating funnel.

Figure 2. A player customizing the look of her in-game avatar.

Unknown to the players (but known to us as designers of the game), the original ammunition substance comprises a mixture of acid and sand. A separating funnel is not an effective piece of apparatus for separating the original mixture as this apparatus works only for immiscible liquids; that is, two liquids that do not dissolve in each other. If a player uses the coarse filter paper (first item from the top in the pane on the left side of Figure 3), she will obtain two derivative substances. (As designers, we know that the two substances are sand, in the filter paper, and acid contaminated with fine sand particles, in the beaker.) When the players encounter the monsters a second time in Level 1 of the game, they will find that their ammunition fares no better than previously if they used the separating funnel. Their weapons jam like before, and their ammunition fares no better than previously against the monsters. Alternatively, if players use the residue in the coarse filter paper (which, unknown to them at this point in time, is composed of sand) as their ammunition, they will find that their weapons now jam even more frequently and their ammunition is totally ineffective against the monsters. Or, if players use the substance collected in the beaker as their ammunition, they will still find their weapons occasionally jamming and their ammunition of greater effectiveness than before but still not sufficiently potent to destroy the monsters (because it contains acid contaminated with fine sand particles). It is only when players use the fine filter paper (second item from top in the left hand pane) to perform the separation technique and furthermore use the now pure acid in the beaker as their ammunition that they will find that their weapons no longer jam and their ammunition is potent enough to destroy the monsters (because the ammunition is now a pure acid and, as it turns out, the monster is made of metal). Assuming that students execute different methods of separation and based on the fact that associated consequences arising from each player's laboratory efforts are made manifest (through battle effectiveness or ineffectiveness) to all players in the second encounter with the monsters, the pressing question that students will face is *why*? For example, why was Mary's ammunition effective in destroying the monsters while John's ammunition was not? What did Mary do in the laboratory that was different from what John did that might account for the different degree of effectiveness observed?

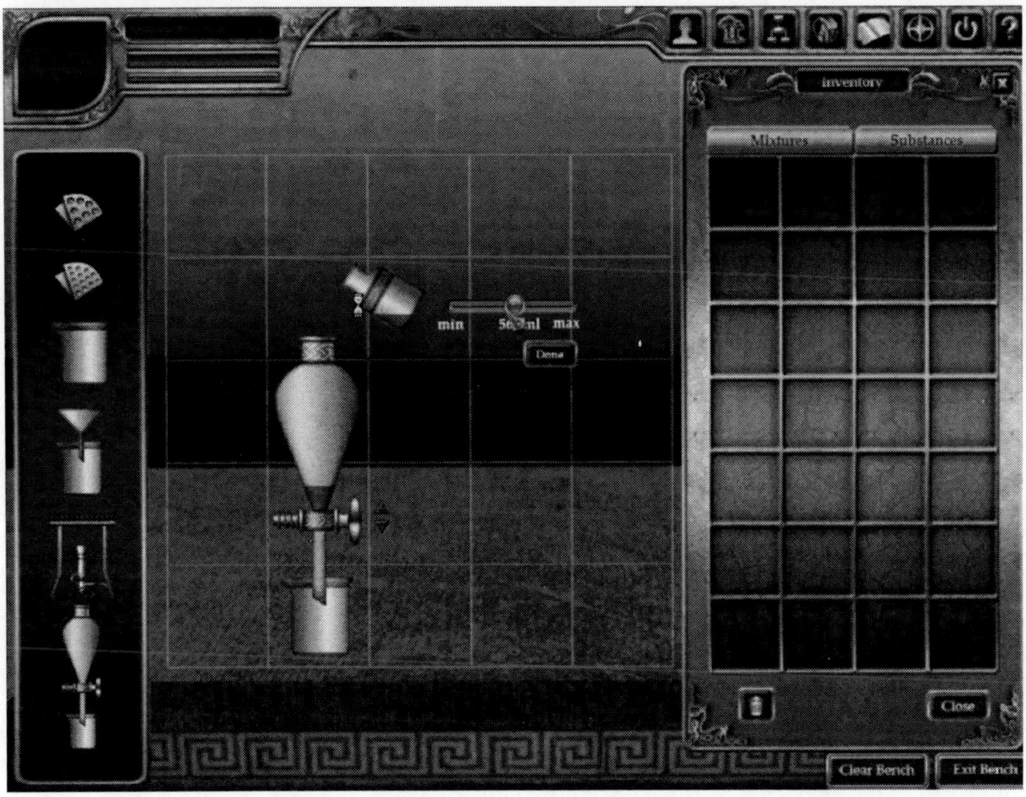

Figure 3. A player performing a chemistry separation technique at the laboratory bench.

The cognitive dissonance generated by students' game play transitions naturally into a classroom space of dialogic learning where they learn with one another to construct the needed answers to their pressing questions. In this process, students engage in making sense of their game experience. They do so by reasoning with one another to establish what different ammunition effects were observed and then working to identify the causal chain of actions that led to the observed effects. This process requires systematic reasoning that employs framing a question for inquiry, constructing hypotheses, running a test of the hypothesis and collecting relevant data, analysing the data or evidence, developing a conceptual model or explanation of what happened, and evaluating the robustness of the model or explanation by developing a causal chain of reasoning that provides a justification for the given explanation. The process parallels the cycle of scientific inquiry that involves questioning, hypothesizing, testing, analysing, modelling, and evaluating.

Although Level 1 game play coupled with the ensuing teacher-facilitated classroom dialog among students may appear simple, it nevertheless serves to illustrate the idea of how students learn chemistry in a performative manner. Student competence in *doing* chemistry is developed through engagement in problem solving and meaning making. These activities are driven by the game narrative. The trajectory of learning that marks students' deepening understanding of chemistry by participating in the *practice* of doing chemistry is referred to as developing "competence-through-performance" in the PDP Model of game-based learning. As students continue playing *Legends of Alkhimia*, the chemistry involved becomes increasingly complex. Like the apprentice scientists that the game positions them to be, students are *required* to develop their own classifications of the substances that they encounter in the game world. They do not experience the world as a pre-labelled and a pre-classified place in contrast to how chemistry textbooks depict chemistry as a *fait accompli.* This pedagogical learning design inducts students into an authentic science practice requiring them to *construct* functional yet parsimonious representations and organizations of knowledge. Examples of such knowledge structures include (1) creating the categories elements, compounds, and mixtures, (2) organizing substances into acids, bases, and salts, as well as (3) classifying elements in the periodic table. As students level up in the game, they are required to continually re-assess the validity and utility of their classifications. These classifications constitute their ontological construction of the game world as experienced through the lens of chemistry, and they will typically undergo revision as more of the game world is experienced and a better fit between the experienced world and the (theoretically) described world is sought. From this perspective, there is no assurance that students will come up with the same set of terms. But this does not matter. What counts is the categorization. So students may choose to call one group of metals 'basic' in the course of their learning. It is a simple matter for the teacher to make the connection to standard vocabulary by informing them that what they refer to as 'basic' is called 'elements' by chemists.

To summarize, the Alkhimia learning program (that is, the program of learning that entails multiple iterations of playing the game and making sense of game play through dialog) instantiates a unique pedagogy of game-based learning that is predicated upon students coming to *know chemistry performatively* by engaging in a fictional game environment that simulates the practice of inquiry. As part of the process, students develop their *own* accounts of the nature of chemistry related phenomena in the first instance. As part of teacher facilitation, students are encouraged to compare their knowledge constructions with those of other students as well as with received constructions of chemistry as a scientific domain. Students then need to argue and negotiate over which account is "best" and provide evidence and justifications for their preferred account. Knowing chemistry in this sense involves much more than just *knowing about* chemistry. Apart from being able to declare propositional assertions *about* the domain (chemistry 'facts'), students also imbibe skills, values, identity, and epistemology related to the doing of chemistry as constituent of scientific practice. As Shaffer (2006) has argued, this is a form of learning that subsumes and integrates skills, knowledge, identity, values, and epistemology. Learning outcomes associated with such pedagogy lead to actionable knowledge, not inert knowledge (Whitehead, 1929). They establish a higher standard for 21st century education.

CONCLUSION

In this chapter, I have critically assessed the pedagogy underlying the design of educational games that are commonly available in the subject domain of chemistry. The finding is that such games lack sophistication due to an overwhelming emphasis on "teaching content." This emphasis reflects a deeper misunderstanding related to the nature of knowledge and of how people come to know. In other words, the problem is epistemological in nature. Many game developers subscribe unwittingly to the fallacy of knowledge possession. Associated with this fallacy, they fail to recognize the inadequacy of knowledge profession, wherein learning is restricted to "talking about" things rather than being able to *do* the things talked about. I have therefore argued for the necessity of knowing through performance. This form of knowing is developed through my Play–Dialog–Performance Model of game-based learning. In this model, learning is sustained in a coherent way to address a substantive and meaningful chunk of ideas such that the ideas become both related and integrated. Students do not master fragmented "knowledge pieces." Instead, they develop a holistic understanding of the target subject domain on the basis of competence-through-performance.

Are schoolteachers, in general, ready to enact the pedagogy of game-based learning in their classrooms? Our research experience to date suggests that there are significant challenges. In concluding this chapter, I shall highlight two challenges. First, it is necessary to recognize that schools are socially and culturally bound spaces. These spaces are characterized by deeply entrenched practices concerning what to teach and how to teach. The instructional concerns are complemented by concerns over what to assess and how to assess, with respect to student learning. Students have also imbibed deep beliefs about what education is from their schooling experience. They understand education in terms of 'acquiring a lot of knowledge' and being assessed on 'whether they have acquired the correct knowledge'. School structures including those of the physical classroom and lesson time tables are resistant to change. In such a context, a reconstruction of expectations and practices is required of both teachers and students if game-based learning is to be enacted successfully. A game-based learning curriculum typically requires time slots of greater duration than is customary in schools. Game playing requires time; post-game dialog requires time. Deep learning processes involving the development of values and identity require time. However, the practice of schooling esteems instructional efficiency and knowledge products much more than student depth of learning and participation in knowledge construction processes. School values are reflected in what is found in assessments of student learning, namely, content knowledge. Consequently, introducing game-based learning into schools creates serious dislocations for both teachers and students. In effect, both stakeholders, amongst others, will need to master a new game of school.

The second challenge that I shall highlight relates to the fact that effective take-up of game-based learning requires a change in epistemological beliefs. Both teachers and students must come to understand and accept that the traditional framing of knowledge, derived from Western philosophy and tracing its roots back to Plato, in terms of 'justified true belief' is severely limiting because its logical and practical outcome is inert knowledge. A performance-oriented criterion, in contrast, empowers the individual and contributes to the creation of productive value in the world. But this outcome is achieved at a greater cost in terms of time and effort. In an age where quick results are valued, the superficiality of the results often goes unnoticed (or is conveniently ignored).

The successful adoption of game-based learning in education will depend on whether stakeholders in the education arena are able to critically discern the state of the enterprise. Openness of thinking and a genuine sense of need for something better are vital ingredients if students are to be given access to a process of education that equips them to deal with life in the 21st century. Will schools rise to the challenge? We surely hope that they will.

AUTHOR INFO

Yam San Chee is an Associate Professor in the Learning Sciences & Technologies Academic Group and the Learning Sciences Lab at the National Institute of Education, Nanyang Technological University, Singapore. He obtained his BSc (Econ) with Honours from the London School of Economics and Political Science, University of London, and his PhD from the University of Queensland, Australia. Prof Chee's research focuses on new literacies and new media in education, with a special emphasis on game-based learning. Recent games developed for research include *Space Station Leonis* and *Escape from Centauri 7*. Current games being developed through NRF funding are *Legends of Alkhimia* and *Statecraft X*. Prof Chee also conducts research on the interaction between online virtual life and real life and how this interaction impacts the construction of self-identity. He was the founding executive editor of *Research and Practice in Technology Enhanced Learning*, the journal of the Asia-Pacific Society for Computers in Education. He is currently an Associate Editor of the *International Journal of Gaming and Computer-Mediated Simulations*.

Associate Professor Yam San CHEE
Learning Sciences & Technologies Academic Group and the Learning Sciences Lab
National Institute of Education, Nanyang Technological University, Singapore
Tel: 65- 67903261
Email: yamsan.chee@nie.edu.sg
Web: http://yamsanchee.home.nie.edu.sg/

ACKNOWLEDGMENTS

The work related to the game *Legends of Alkhimia* is funded by research grant NRF2007–IDM005–MOE–006 funded by the National Research Foundation of Singapore and administered by the Ministry of Education. I wish to gratefully acknowledge the contributions of the following team members participating in the Alkhimia project: Daniel Tan, Tan Ek Ming, Rahul Nath, Wee Yik Shan, Ong Cher Yee, Ho Won Kit, Henry Kang, and Ittirat Vayachut.

References

Abt, C. C. (1970). *Serious games*. New York: Viking Press.

Bakhtin, M. M. (1981). *The dialogic imagination: Four essays*. Austin, TX: University of Texas Press.

Bartlett, F. C. (1932). *Remembering: A study in experimental and social psychology*. Cambridge, UK: Cambridge University Press.

Berger, P., & Luckmann, T. (1966). *The social construction of reality: A treatise in the sociology of knowledge*. London: Penguin Books.

Chee, Y. S. (2002). Refocusing learning on pedagogy in a connected world. *On the Horizon, 10*(4), 7–13.

Chee, Y. S. (in preparation). Play, dialog, and performance: The PDP model of game-based learning.

Chee, Y. S., Tan, E. M., & Lee, J. L. H. (2010). Learning with computer games: Beyond mastering subject content. In C. S. Chai & Q. Wang (Eds.), *ICT for self-directed and collaborative learning* (pp. 366–382). Singapore: Prentice-Hall.

Damasio, A. (1994). *Descartes' error: Emotion, reason, and the human brain*. New York: Penguin Books.

Dewey, J. (1938/1991). *Logic: The theory of inquiry* (Vol. 12, The Later Works of John Dewey, 1925–1953). Carbondale, IL: Southern Illinois University Press.

Gagnon, G. W. J., & Collay, M. (2006). *Constructivist learning design*. Thousand Oaks, CA: Corwin Press.

Garrison, J. W. (1998). John Dewey's philosophy as education. In L. A. Hickman (Ed.), *Reading Dewey: Interpretations for a postmodern generation* (pp. 63–81). Bloomington, IN: Indiana University Press.

Geertz, C. (1973). *The interpretation of cultures*. New York: Basic Books.

Gergen, K. J. (1994). *Realities and relationships*. Cambridge, MA: Harvard University Press.

Gergen, K. J. (1999). *An invitation to social construction*. London, UK: Sage.

Hayakawa, S. I., & Hayakawa, A. R. (1990). *Language in thought and action* (5th ed.). San Diego, CA: Harcourt Brace.

Hickman, L. A. (1998). Dewey's theory of inquiry. In L. A. Hickman (Ed.), *Reading Dewey: Interpretations for a postmodern generation* (pp. 166–186). Bloomington, IN: Indiana University Press.

Klages, M. (2006). *Literary theory: A guide for the perplexed*. London, UK: Contiunnum.

Korzybski, A. (1994). *Science and sanity: An introduction to non-Aristotelian systems and general semantics* (5th ed.). Englewood, NJ: Institute of General Semantics.

Lakoff, G., & Johnson, M. (1980). *Metaphors we live by*. Chicago, IL: University of Chicago Press.

Masciotra, D., Roth, W.-M., & Morel, D. (2007). *Enaction: Toward a Zen mind in learning and teaching*. Rotterdam: Sense Publishers.

Minick, N. (1987). The development of Vygotsky's thought: An introduction. In R. W. Rieber & A. S. Carton (Eds.), *The collected works of L. S. Vygotsky* (Vol. 1). New York: Plenum.

Newell, A. (1982). The knowledge level. *Artificial Intelligence, 18*, 87–127.

Postman, N., & Weingartner, C. (1969). *Teaching as a subversive activity*. New York: Dell Publishing.

Prensky, M. (2001). *Digital game-based learning*. New York: McGraw-Hill.

Prensky, M. (2007). "Don't bother me, Mom–I'm learning": How computer and video games are preparing your kids for 21st century success. Retrieved August 28, 2009, from http://www.k12schoolnetworking.org/2007/symposium/presentations/PrenskyGamesandSimulations.pdf

Rosenfield, I. (1988). *The invention of memory: A new view of the brain*. New York: Basic Books.

Schechner, R. (2003). *Performance theory* (2nd ed.). New York: Routledge.

Schechner, R. (2006). *Performance studies: An introduction* (2nd ed.). New York: Routledge.

Shaffer, D. W. (2006). *How computer games help children learn*. New York: Palgrave Macmillan.

Smith, P. L., & Ragan, T. J. (1999). *Instructional Design* (2nd ed.). Upper Saddle River, NJ: Prentice-Hall.

Thwaites, T., Davis, L., & Mules, W. (2002). *Introducing cultural and media studies: A semiotic approach*. Basingstoke, UK: Palgrave.

Wells, G. (1999). *Dialogic inquiry: Towards a socio-cultural practice and theory of education*. New York: Cambridge University Press.

Whitehead, A. N. (1929). *The aims of education*. New York: Macmillan.

Zyda, M. (2005). From visual simulation to virtual reality to games. *IEEE Computer, 38*(9), 25–32.

In: Interactive and Digital Media for Education in Virtual … ISBN: 978-1-61668-844-8
Editor: Cai Yiyu

Chapter 2

SIMULATING A "REAL" WORLD OR PLAYING A GAME? STUDENTS PLAYING A COTS GAME IN THE SCIENCE CLASSROOM

Elisabet M. Nilsson and Gunilla Svingby
School of Education, Malmö University, Sweden

ABSTRACT

Thirty students aged 13-15 were observed at school when playing the COTS computer game SimCity 4 with the mission to create sustainable cities. The aim was to study students' use of scientific concepts, theories, and processes during gameplay. The analysis demonstrates that the gaming students were engaged in what can be described as scientific practice. They were exploring, penetrating and manipulating the game mechanics, thus demonstrating an understanding of the interdependency of factors in the system. This was, however, mostly done in a rather unsystematic way. Students did observe and discuss the results of their actions, and according to later decisions also learned from them, but formal analyses or conclusions were largely lacking. They treated the gameplay as part of the school task, and the game as a virtual dynamic system rather than as a simulated real world. The results illustrate the assumption that computer gameplay in school needs to be contextualised in a way that enables the students to make sense of the educationally relevant content.

Keywords: Computer games, SimCity 4, learning, scientific practice, observation studies

INTRODUCTION: COMPUTER GAMEPLAY IN SCIENCE LEARNING CONTEXTS

The educational potential of computer games is theoretically well founded, assuming that computer games in themselves are powerful educational tools (e.g. Egenfeldt-Nielsen, 2007; Gee, 2003). It is argued that games can constitute models of environments for learning practices since "they lower the threat of failure; foster a sense of engagement through immersion; sequence tasks to allow early success; link learning to goals and roles; create social context; are multi-modal; support early steps into a domain" (Dibley & Parish, 2007, p. 35). Games designed according to acknowledged research on learning "can help establish a narrative, perceptual, and social world[s]" (Barab et al., 2007b, p. 752) that invite students to *play with identities*, move outside the student role in the classroom, and into the role of an active participant stakeholder. Additionally, such games may provide students with *challenges* that are problem based and meaningful in the context of the game world, implying that the game world provides students with a sense of intentionality and consequentiality. Of specific relevance for science education, Squire and Jan (2007) state that computer games can be thought of as *contested spaces*, where there is a spatially bound problem which changes over time, depending on students' actions in the game. This type of game allows for the embedding of *authentic resources*, and tools critical to success in the gameplay. Empirical studies on educational games especially designed for use in science classrooms provide grounded support for these claims (e.g. Barab et al., 2007a, 2007b; Ketelhut, 2007; Magnussen, 2008; Nelson et al., 2005; Squire & Jan, 2007; Squire & Klopfer, 2007).

It is argued that computer games provide dynamic representations, offering gamers embodied experiences in complex domains that are otherwise difficult to access (e.g. Barab et al., 2007a, 2007b; Neulight et al., 2007; Squire & Klopfer, 2007). Empirical research suggests that computer games can function as potential providers of dynamic representations of real world situations, where scientific experiments are executed to help students move from scientific content to scientific experience (e.g. Mathevet et al., 2007; Nelson et al., 2005; Neulight et al., 2007). At the same time, research also shows that the link between the representation and what it represents is not always made by the gamer, and that children playing games do not necessarily treat games as a representation of something outside of the game (Linderoth, 2004).

Also commonly brought forward is the assumption that learning and the intrinsic motivation of fun are intimately connected (e.g. Hansmann et al., 2005; Malone 1981). However, a number of studies demonstrate that the fact that playing is "fun" does not automatically bring about learning (Lim et al., 2006; Rehn et al., 2007; Rieber & Noah, 2008; Sim et al., 2006). An example of this is a study conducted in the UK on the use of commercial off-the-shelf (COTS) games[1] in schools. The outcome implies that using games in lessons is motivating, but may not always motivate students to learn the subject content (Sandford et al., 2006).

Results presented by Sandford et al. (2006), Price (2008), and Van Eck (2006) indicate that it remains difficult to draw clear conclusions concerning the effects of using COTS games in science education. In comparison to educational computer games, few studies have explored the potentials of playing COTS games in science classrooms (Svingby & Nilsson, In progress). One example is the study by Price (2008), exploring if the physics engine of Unreal Tournament 2004[2] could be used for physics education. The study demonstrates that the physics engine is in fact capable of supporting experiments; that qualitative experiments developed with UT 2004 have positive impacts on students' learning of physics, and that it supports collaboration. Also stated is that since the game is primarily designed to provide

[1] The Sims 2 (Maxis, 2004), Knights of Honor (Crytek Black Sea, 2004) and RollerCoaster Tycoon 3 (Frontier Developments, 2004) were the games played in the study.

[2] Epic Games, 2004.

gaming experiences, the game mechanics carry pedagogical limitations, which should be considered if the game is used in schools. Another study (Van Eck, 2006) explores the potential of various COTS games[3] played in the classroom to change students' attitudes toward technology, mathematics and science. The study shows that playing the games had a positive impact on attitudes, and that girls, in particular, might be encouraged to find technology more relevant. It was also observed that girls' and boys' gaming strategies greatly vary. For example, when playing SimSafari[4], "the girls tended to build dwellings complete with bathrooms, hot tubs, and pools; boys, on the other hand, tended to create swamps, crocodiles, and jaguars to the exclusion of everything else" (Van Eck, 2006, p. 5).

SimCity (Maxis, 2003) is an example of a COTS game that frequently has been played in classrooms (e.g. Adams 1998; Gaber 2007; Euström & Hofverberg, 2006; Lauwert, 2007, Nilsson & Jakobsson, Submitted). Research generally reports favourably, stating that the gameplay enables "group discussion and experimentation", and "often facilitate[s] a wider range of skills than immediately apparent from the game" (Kirriemuir & McFarlan, 2004, p. 24). Examples of skills referred to include "mathematical skills, urban planning, economics, engineering, environmental awareness" (p. 24). Gaber (2007) puts forward two clearly identified cognitive learning objectives when using simulation computer games, such as SimCity. The first is *holistic understanding*, which implies an ability to see that a situation is embedded in a larger context, and that the whole consists of many interconnected parts. Through such insights, the students develop strategic knowledge, and an understanding that their decisions may not only have a direct impact on the immediate situation, but also consequential impacts on other, not directly linked situations. The second learning objective is adaptive *critical reasoning*, implying that when students are allowed to manipulate variables in a simulation computer game, they develop critical reasoning skills that may be used to solve problems.

Nevertheless, certain pedagogical limitations inhered in the game are also pointed out. One limitation brought up is the fact that SimCity "embeds very specific ideas about the American city", (Lauwaert, 2007, p. 197). The game mechanics demand growth and change in order to become successful. More sustainable city types, where other human or ecological needs are given priority, are not represented, or possible to simulate. Despite pedagogical limitations, the study by Euström and Hofverberg (2006) concludes that the content embedded in SimCity is in line with parts of the Swedish Science curriculum. They state that playing the game may support science learning, but that the outcome depends on what educators do to facilitate this process. Students' responses in a questionnaire, maintaining that they played the game quite differently when at home, supports the conclusion that the game does not facilitate science learning in itself. Instead, learning is achieved through gaming activities in combination with off-game discussions, and investigations.

The empirical study presented in this chapter investigates use of SimCity 4[5] in the classroom. SimCity is a single player computer game, where the gamer plays the role of a

---

[3] Games played: Rockett's New School (Purple Moon, 1997), Nancy Drew (Her Interactive, 1998), The Mystery of the Nautilus (Cryo Interactive, 2001), Monkey Island (LucasArt, 1990), Mysterious Journey — Schizm (Avalon, 2001), Battlezone (Atari, 1980), Backyard Soccer (Humongous Entertainment, 2001), SimSafari (Maxis, 1998), Dinotopia (Dinotopia, 2003).

[4] Maxis, 1998.

[5] From now on simply referred to as "SimCity". Information about the game is taken from Electronic Arts' Overview of SimCity (EA.com, 2009) [2009-08-28].

mayor, with the mission to create and manage a city populated by contented citizens. When starting to play, the first steps are to shape the landscape, placing zones, laying out a grid structure for residential, commercial or industrial development, installing public services (e.g. power, water, transport systems, health care, education, safety, leisure). A variety of energy supply systems are afforded: coal power plant, hydrogen power plant, natural gas power plant, nuclear power plant, oil power plant, solar power plant, waste-to-energy plant, and windmills. Not all of the alternatives are available initially, since some have requirements that go with them. Information concerning such requirements, costs, and level of environmental quality is available in the game.

The key to creating a successful city is to maintain balance between various factors, such as a growing population, urban and economic development, environmental disturbances, and quality of life for its citizens. As the city matures and grows, new possibilities appear, as well as the need for additional services. The city gradually turns into a more complex system, with many different factors that determine its progress. Visual feedback on the state of the city is constantly provided through various signs that indicate problems, for example, crowds, piles of trash, traffic congestion. Also data views and graphs indicating levels of pollution, crime, education, traffic situation, and garbage disposal can be accessed on request. Now and then, virtual "advisors" appear, drawing attention to problems and accomplishments in the game.

SimCity could be seen as a tool for *simulated science practice* (Future City, 2008; Euström & Hofverberg, 2006). Such practice may involve: observation of a system (here the simulated city); formulation of a hypothesis to explain the observations of the system; prediction of the behaviour of the system; experiments to test the validity of the hypothesis. Aitkin (2004), among others, argues that "scientific knowledge consists of both knowledge about a system, and knowledge of how to investigate the system" (p. 248). This *how-to* knowledge cannot be gained solely or even primarily from reading about science, but must be gained from actually practicing science. Simulations are used by scientists as scientific tools, and simulation games may be used for similar purposes.

To be engaged in scientific processes includes "describing, explaining and predicting scientific phenomena; understanding scientific investigation; interpreting scientific evidence and conclusions" (OECD, 2003, p. 133). Aitkin believes that the actual process of "puzzle-solving" involved in science practice takes place in the same way during gameplay "involving cycles of action, observation, reflection and theorising" (2004, p. 248). In gameplay this engagement includes exploring, penetrating and manipulating the dynamic systems that the game mechanics constitute. In such processes of system thinking, problems are looked upon as part of the overall system, and the only way to understand why a problem occurs is to put it in relation to the whole (O' Connor, 1997). The question is if playing SimCity in the classroom context spurs such processes?

COMPUTER GAMEPLAY IN SWEDEN

When it comes to computers Swedish homes are well equipped[6], and most families have one or more computers. Two thirds of the Swedish girls and boys in the ages 12-16 years

[6] Statistics Sweden. <www.scb.se> [2009-08-28]

access Internet on a daily basis for online gaming, chatting, watching film clips, engaging in social communities, doing school work etc. (Swedish Media Council, 2008). Computer gameplay is a significant activity. Most boys (96%), and more than two thirds of the girls (71%) play computer games regularly (ibid.). The same is, however, not true for schools. Even if the supply of computers in schools is fairly high (six students/computer, ages 7-16, and 2 ½ students/computer, ages 16-19), the computers are not always easily accessed and may lack technical support (Swedish National Agency for Education, 2009). Half of the teachers questioned report that they use computers during class at least once a week.

The National Agency for Education's (2009) report does not reveal what kind of computer-supported tools teachers apply, and no comprehensive nation-wide study on the usage of computer games in Swedish schools exists today. Smaller studies indicate, however, that computer games are used primarily for language and mathematics learning, and as a reward in lower grades (Ljung-Djärf, 2004). The games used are simple skills games. A recent initiative to promote the use of computer games in schools is directed towards teacher training by a network, aiming at, among other things, the integration of computer gameplay in the teacher education curriculum (National Network for ICT in Teacher Education). Another initiative worth mentioning is Future City (Future City, 2008), which is an annual competition for Swedish schools and students aged 12-15, organised by private organisations (within the building trade). In teams, students take on the role of urban planners with the mission to create sustainable cities, handling matters such as the infrastructure, building constructions, transport system, and power supply. The competition is divided into three components: (1) to design and visualise a city in SimCity; (2) to build a physical model of a section of the city created in SimCity; and (3) to make a written and oral presentation of the assumptions underlying design choices. Future City has been running in Sweden since 2003. In the school year 2008/2009 2,200 students from 52 schools were enrolled in the competition.

The situation in Sweden is similar to that of Denmark, a country that has been part of a European study of the use of games in schools (European Schoolnet, 2009). Even if a majority of teachers state that they use both COTS and educational computer games in their teaching, the use of computer games is not regarded as common practice in Denmark, or in any other of the European countries in the study (Austria, France, Italy, Lithuania, the Netherlands, Spain, UK). A majority of the teachers involved in the study requested more information about the potentials, and practices of using computer games in the classroom.

Two Swedish Studies

Study I: Students' Reflections on Creating Future Cities in a Computer Game

In a recent study of SimCity, students' use of scientific concepts and formalism was studied, as well as their apprehension of the realism of the game (Nilsson & Jakobsson, Submitted). The game was played during students' participation in the national competition Future City (Future City, 2008) with the mission to create sustainable cities. Students were interviewed after their participation, and their retrospective reflections on the strategies applied during the gameplay when choosing an energy supply system were analysed. 42

students in eleven groups from four different schools participated. The outcome of the study demonstrates how the students consciously considered, and used various kinds of gaming strategies to attain the aim of a sustainable city. Three major strategies were observed.

The strategy referred to in the following as the *Green path*, meant implementing the most environmentally friendly alternative from the start, by choosing renewable sources of energy. The strategy resulted in slow industrial development, slow expansion of population, less income from taxes, and a low level of pollution. From a game perspective, this may be classified as a less successful strategy, even though it was successful from the viewpoint of building a sustainable society. Students who chose this strategy were clearly disadvantaged in the game world, which resulted in a situation, where their city described a slow development and offered limited possibilities for action.

Students applying the strategy *Industrial growth* used cost efficient, but environmentally less friendly energy systems, resulting in the generation of power at low costs, but in high levels of pollution. This strategy resulted in overall growth; industrial development, and many citizens moving in. The strategy allowed for the generation of high incomes at an early stage, making it possible to later on invest in better energy alternatives. The initial use of power plants based on fossil fuels, in order to reach economic development, thus provided the basis for later large investments in more environmentally friendly alternatives.

The third strategy, *Cheats*, meant that students took advantage of weaknesses in the game mechanics (referred to as *exploits*, Salen, 2004), finding loopholes and ways of getting around the game restraints. This strategy increased the city budget, allowing large investment more quickly, and was above all used to create possibilities to build environmentally friendly alternatives. Although the strategy may be referred to as "cheating", it can also be seen as the demonstration of creative ability and competence of being able to penetrate a dynamic system, and make the most out of it, in order to fulfil the purpose of the activity.

Even though the two first strategies follow different logic and preferences regarding the importance of the economy versus environmental sustainability, both demonstrate long term planning, strategic thinking and an understanding of the complex game system. In addition, the third group also demonstrates the ability to manipulate the game systems, in order to reach their aim of creating both a sustainable city, and a city that attracted money and inhabitants. The gameplay thus indicates high skills in system thinking, and demonstrates understanding of a complex technical system, as well as knowledge of how manipulation of one part affects another part of the system.

Students were, on the whole, critical of the limitations set by the game mechanics, preventing them from implementing their own ideas. Students were also critical of the values inbuilt in the game, to the effect that the success of every action depended on the economy. The interviews additionally showed that when asked to reflect on their cities, participants were able to explicitly explain how they had applied scientific concepts and theories, sometimes using adequate scientific language, but more often using everyday words. For example, some students were able to use concepts like "photosynthesis", "carbon dioxide", and "greenhouse gases" in an adequate way when explaining air pollution. On the other hand, when reflecting on their cities and discussing their strategies, students' misunderstandings concerning the involved concepts and the underlying theories were also exposed.

The study demonstrates that the game can provide a science learning context, where students are allowed to apply and contextualise their scientific knowledge, by manipulating variables in a system, as well as experiencing consequences of their actions.

Study II: "Simply" Playing SimCity, or Engaging in Scientific Practice?

The results reported above were based on interviews made after the game was played; that is, the rationale for the gamers' choices was formulated once the physical model had already been built (a part of Future City), and the proposal had been submitted. The formulation of their strategies and other results indicated by the study were most probably the result of the whole context, including the thinking provoked by the interviewer's questions. The study, thus, did not reflect the precise part the gameplay had in the results, nor did it illuminate the question of how (if) students applied science practice.

With the aim of shedding light on these issues, an observation study was conducted. The study was guided by the following assumptions and questions.

- How (if) scientific processes were applied, when SimCity was played in schools with the aim of creating an environmentally sustainable city, and if strategies like the above emerged by playing.
- When a dynamic system is explored and manipulated, upcoming problems are treated as part of the overall system, and are related to the system as a whole. The study focused on how (if) students during gameplay treated the problems that emerged in the city as part of the system as a whole.
- Since "immersiveness" is a fundamental characteristic of "good" games[7], the study was also directed towards observing to what extent students were immersed when playing. In what ways were the students critically commenting on the internal premises, the restraints and biases built in the framework of the game?

Figure 1. Gaming student groups in action.

[7] See e.g. Gee (2003).

The study involved 30 students (14 girls and 16 boys, aged 13-15), all at the same school, and by the educator divided in four groups (see Figure 1). Students played during the time scheduled for the Future City competition. The activity was part of the students' self-managed project work. The scheduling of the sessions was organised by students themselves, and only to a limited extent supervised by a teacher. The school had dedicated three weeks to the playing of SimCity, and the observation study was conducted during the last week of this period.

FOUR GROUPS PLAYING SIMCITY

The observation of the four gaming groups identified the following strategies.

GROUP A: Practicing Scientific and System Thinking. Economy and Environment

The gameplay seemed to be directed by the idea of building a sustainable city. For example, decisions concerning the location and choice of industries and energy supply system were discussed in relation to their environmental impact. Nevertheless, the economy worked as the main tool when creating the energy supply system. The group started with natural gas power plants because they were cheap. Later on, they invested in solar power plants, but then went back to nature gas power plants, since the solar power plants had a negative influence on the economy of the city. However, even though they made these changes the power problems remained. A student said "I don't get it, there is something with the power, I build three new power plants but there is still power failure"[8], and continued "because of the power failures people couldn't pump water, and without water and power people start moving out and we lose tax income". The gameplay was characterised by system thinking. They traced the causes of problems that occur on the screen, and discussed how problems may be solved.

Graphs and charts for levels for pollutions, level of education and so on were continuously checked. The possibilities to experiment offered within the game were used by the students to experience the underlying system, and the interdependency of various parts. Students talked of matters linked to pollution, and environmentally friendly solutions. Only when discussing choice of energy supply system did they apply some formal language.

Students related events in the game to experiences in the real world, for example, when discussing nuclear power plants in the game and in the Swedish context, or when relating problems of pollution to areas in their home town. The students also commented on the game mechanics, for example by challenging the limitations set by the framework, which hampered more environmentally friendly solutions. Students commented that the game is not "logical", since there is no logical relation between the size of the space and the number of citizens. One of the students pinpointed that the game is a "city simulation" not a "citizens simulation".

To this group, playing the game obviously provoked questions and offered possibilities for learning. Having played for some time, the group stated that the city was not good

[8] All student quotes are by the authors translated from Swedish to English.

enough. To try to build a more environmentally friendly city, they started over again (from where they had last saved the game), this time avoiding the same mistakes.

GROUP B: Playing Towards a Goal by the Game Rules. Experiences used for Learning

The group started creating a new city from scratch according to the idea of building a sustainable city. Their first move was to plant trees, a move that was motivated by the experience of earlier play that the planting of trees resulted in reduced air pollution levels which eventually were going to increase when the city expanded. Also, when placing the zones they were referring to what is "to come". One student explained that they placed the industrial zones far from the residential zones since "they [the citizens moving in] prefer to live there and have clean air". The group when playing seemed to be guided by a long term goal, rather than by immediate gains. The students created the city in a systematic way, adding new elements whenever the information offered by the game, via graphs and other statistics, indicated needs and possibilities. Instead of reacting directly on what was happening in the game at any given moment, students manipulated the dynamic system as part of a strategy. It may be said that the students thereby adopted a form of scientific practice.

Experiences of what happened when a specific solution was chosen for the previous city were now used as "experimental data", in forming a "hypothesis" directing the design of their present city. The group made conscious experiments. When the game indicated high levels of air pollution, the students tested the effects of planting trees, and used the information gained in consecutive moves. This way the students demonstrated growing knowledge of the game as a system.

On the whole, the game was played according to the embedded game rules. From the start, the group deliberately chose to invest in natural gas, since this energy source was relatively cheap, and was considered quite environmentally friendly. When the economy got better, the students chose instead to install solar power. The change was motivated by the environmental benefits. The choice was preceded by a discussion of effects versus costs of various energy systems. Even if the group played with the intention of creating an environmentally friendly city, they did not use scientific concepts when discussing the alternatives. Nor did they discuss the underlying scientific content at any depth, or referred more than occasionally to similar situations in their own home town. The gameplay seemed, however, to bring out a number of problems and questions that the students were aware of and had some prior knowledge of. The concrete experience of trying to build what they knew as "sustainable energy systems", and failing because of the inbuilt significance of the city economy in the game, led to discussions of the relative importance of various factors, and to strategies to overcome the restrictions built into the game. The students did not, however, explicitly comment on the underlying game mechanics.

GROUP C: Playing a Game

The group started to build a new city, since they had rejected all of their previous attempts.

Since they had been building a number of cities, they were well aware of how the game mechanics worked, and how to make "use" of it. The economic parameters were the primary source of the students' actions in the game. Now and then, students discussed moral and social aspects of the alternatives offered by the game, but in the end economic factors determined what actions to carry through. An example was the decision to build a missile industry to earn extra money, or trying to get rid of poor people by making them move to another city. The playing was obviously steered by a wish to "win" the game, by choosing moves that resulted in as many "gains" as possible. The students demonstrated that they understood how the game parameters were connected, for example, education in relation to productivity. This was for example made obvious when a student was explaining that "farming is good for the health, but if you only have agriculture they [the citizens] skip school, because it [education] is not needed". Another example was when the executor chose to invest in a lot of stores since they do not pollute and in the longer run provide a lot of job opportunities for the citizens.

When playing, they used their earlier experiences of playing the game, and talked about "smart moves", and mistakes to be avoided. The observation demonstrated clearly that the group played the game as a school task. They did not get immersed into the story, and they did not relate the gameplay to problems encountered in the real world. No scientific knowledge was referred to or noticeable during the game, except when choosing an energy supply system.

GROUP D: Ad Hoc. No Scientific Formalism and No System Thinking

The gameplay was characterised by reactions to immediate upcoming problems, such as citizens moving away, or the outbreak of fires. There seemed to be no plan in the actions taken, only reactions to what was happening on the screen. The city economy seemed to be the most important parameter for the actions taken.

Students seldom referred to any scientific content, or system. One student on some occasions asked questions dealing with the environment, for example, about recycling stations. Other students occasionally recommended a move with environmentally friendly arguments, like "can we put high tech things in the centre? Yes, they do not pollute, and they save travel time", and "You will not be able to build high tech things ...it may be some polluting shit. We do not want that, in that case we have to remove it". No discussions took place concerning the strategy and arguments for the energy supply system that was chosen. Students never brought up the possibility of changing their existing energy supply system to a more environmentally friendly alternative, and did not discuss possible environmental consequences.

Despite the overall absence of reasoning based on scientific arguments, the students demonstrated an understanding of the interconnections of the game system itself, and adjusted their moves accordingly commenting on consequences of their actions, and balancing between factors. On the whole, the students in this group expressed little direct criticism towards the game mechanics. Nevertheless, one of the girls once complained about the citizens' passive approach, thus indirectly criticizing the game mechanics. The same girl questioned the game rules implying that citizens had to replace facilities like a train station only because it had grown old, which also indicates a criticism towards the values embedded in the game.

CONCLUSIONS

Students were observed at school, when playing the COTS game SimCity as part of the competition Future City, with the aim of supporting students' knowledge of complex systems by letting them manipulate, and experiment with urban planning. The cities were to be environmentally sustainable.

Our analysis demonstrates that when playing the students were engaged in what can be described as a form of scientific practice. They were exploring, penetrating and manipulating the game mechanics, thus demonstrating understanding of the interdependency of factors in the system. This was, however, mostly done in a rather unsystematic way. Students did observe and discuss the results of their actions to some extent. According to later decisions it appears that they also learned from these experiences, but formal analyses or conclusions were largely lacking. The gaming strategies used were tightly connected to the game mechanics that SimCity builds upon.

As in all kinds of cultural products, certain cultural values are embedded in SimCity. "Successful" gameplay demands continuous growth and change. Property value (influenced by factors such as distance to the city centre, parks, water, level of pollution, crime rates) is a crucial factor in this process. A more sustainable city, where ecological needs are given priority, is basically not allowed by the prerequisites set by the game mechanics. Lauwert (2007) points to three built-in biases in internal logics of the game: "(a) the fact that the game only offers zoned and thus sprawling urban development options to the player, (b) thereby excluding other visions on urban development (most notably those of New Urbanism), and (c) its tribute to the principles of California's realpolitik as practices during the 1980s" (p. 197). This is made visible by the interconnections between development, property taxes, crime and the environment. In order to become a successful mayor of SimCity, gamers ought to keep city taxes low, and strive for high property value levels, as well as low crime rates. Lauwert describes the game as a kind of "machine for commerce" (p. 197); pragmatic, functional, and expanding according to material needs. Other types of cities are not possible to simulate.

The game mechanisms obviously influenced the groups. While playing, students did not focus on scientific formalism, but on actually solving the problem of building a sustainable city by acting upon the affordances offered within the rules framework of the game. To reach the goal of a sustainable future city, the groups chose various strategies, trying not to interfere with the game mechanics. The main discussion between students, thus, dealt with how to obtain balance within the game system. Both direct and indirect criticisms towards the premises of the game world were expressed. When trying alternative solutions, students in all groups challenged the limitations set by the game mechanics. One group complained of the logics of the game mechanisms. Students also commented on the inbuilt value system, saying that the game only offers today's solutions, thereby preventing the building of a city for the future.

The study demonstrates some important aspects of computer games in relation to science education: like scientists, gamers are motivated by the desire to solve problems. Gamers act upon the game world with the intention of accomplishing their goals. They observe the effects these actions have, reflect on the divergence between what they tried to produce and what actually happened, and thereafter formulate and implement new strategies (Aitkin, 2004). Further, the majority of systems that scientists study are not readily accessible, because of their size and complexity. SimCity and other computer games offer the possibility of simulation of such systems, in a form that provides control and safety. The game also provides visualisation and interactivity, not provided by ordinary school books.

The question of immersion is of interest in this context. Students occasionally got very engaged in the game, but they were not immersed into it. They treated the gameplay as part of the school task, and the game as a virtual dynamic system, rather than as a simulated real world. Baker et al. (2008) refers to this as a phenomenon of "gaming the system", where students attempt to succeed in an educational environment by exploiting the properties of that system, rather than learning the embedded material. During gameplay, no attention was, for example, paid to the citizens, and how they would react if this was a real world situation. Students rarely related occurrences happening in the game world to situations in the real world. On the other hand, students were highly engaged. They tried out solutions, and criticised the game mechanics.

The game obviously worked as a simulation context for urban planning (and scientific inquiry, for example, when choosing a power supply system) but with an inbuilt bias that was not accepted by the students. This tension might have been used by the teacher for reflection and discussion. In the first study reported, the focus group interviews worked this way, by engaging students in elaborating on their actions in the game, and reflecting on the consequences of the actions. The interview situation was in some respects similar to a classroom discussion following an inquiry project. In the second study, no such initiative was taken, since the aim was to simply observe the gaming students, interfering as little as possible.

The results of the first and the second study reported here illustrate the assumption that educational use of computer games ought to be seen as interplay between game, student, context, and educator. In accordance with previous research (e.g. Egenfeldt-Nielsen, 2007), it can be stated that if computer games are to be used in the classroom educators need to be fully engaged in the procedure (in similarity to any other pedagogical tool). The educator ought to plan for lessons where students are invited to reflect, summarise and draw conclusions, thus connecting the experiences of playing the game to science, and relating scientific formalism to the actual game context (e.g. Barab et al., 2007a, 2007b; Nelson, 2005). That is, computer gameplay in the classroom needs to be contextualised in a way that enables the students to make sense of the educationally relevant content.

Recent studies of educators' attitudes toward using computer games in school, report of both rather positive attitudes from most teachers but at the same time of a feeling of not knowing where to find "good" computer games, and what to do with them (e.g. Williamson, 2009). So far, rather few studies investigating the educator's role in learning settings involving computer games have been conducted, and in particular when it comes to the use of COTS games (Svingby & Nilsson, In progress). Even though such games are the games most frequently used by teachers in classrooms few researchers have studied learning outcomes, and/or interactions with teaching. This lack of research results, as well as the outcome of the two empirical studies presented in this chapter indicate a need for more research on how COTS games can be integrated into the science curriculum taking advantage of both the unique qualities of these kinds of games, and of the educators' competence.

AUTHORS INFO

Elisabet M. Nilsson holds a Ph.D. in Educational Sciences from the School of Education, Malmö University in Sweden.Dr Gunilla Svingby is professor at the School of Education, Malmö University and co-founder of Malmö University Center for Games Studies.

Corresponding Author
Elisabet M. Nilsson
School of Education
Malmö University
205 06 Malmö, Sweden
Email: elisabet.nilsson@mah.se
Phone: + 46 706 03 36 96
Fax: + 46 40 665 81 40
Web: www.mah.se

REFERENCES

Adams, P. C. (1998). Teaching and Learning with SimCity 2000. *Journal of Geography,* 97(2), 47–55.

Aitkin, A. L. (2004). *Playing at Reality: Exploring the potential of the digital game as a medium for science communication.* Doctoral Thesis. Melbourne: Faculty of Science, The Australian National University.

Baker, R. S.; Walonoski, J.; Heffernan, N.; Roll, I.; Corbett, A. T. & Koedinger, K. R. (2008). Why Students Engage in "Gaming the System" Behavior in Interactive Learning Environments. *Journal of Interactive Learning Research*, 19(2), 185–224.

Barab, S. A.; Sadler, T. D.; Heiselt, C.; Hickey, D. & Zuiker, S. (2007a). Relating Narrative, Inquiry, and Inscriptions: Supporting Consequential Play. *Journal of Science Education and Technology*, 16 (1), 59–82.

Barab, S. A.; Zuiker, S.; Warren, S.; Hickey, D.; Ingram-Goble, A.; & Kwon, E. J. (2007b). Situationally Embodied Curriculum: Relating Formalisms and Contexts. *Science Education*, 91(5), 750–782.

Dibley, J. & Parish, J. (2007). Using Video Games to Understand Thermoregulation. *Science Scope,* 8(30), 32–25.

Egenfeldt-Nielsen, S. (2007). *Educational potential of computer games*. London: Continuum.

European, S. (2009). *How are digital games used in schools?*. Brussels: European Schoolnet. games.eun.org

Euström, A. & Hofverberg, L. (2006). *Kommersiella datorspel, en studie av SimCity i undervisningen (Commercial of-the-shelf computer games, A study of SimCity in formal education).* Bachelor's essay. Malmö: Malmö University.

Future City (2008). *Handbok till Future City 2008/2009.* Stockholm: Future City. www.futurecity.nu

Gaber, J. (2007). Simulating Planning: SimCity as a Pedagogical Tool. *Journal of Planning Education and Research,* 27(2), 113–121.

Hansmann, R., Scholz, R. W., Francke, Carl-Johan A. C. & Weymann, M. (2005). Enhancing environmental awareness: Ecological and economic effects of food consumption. *Simulation & Gaming*, 36(3), 364–382.

Ketelhut, D. J. (2007). The Impact of Student Self-efficacy on Scientific Inquiry Skills: An Exploratory Investigation in River City, a Multi-user Virtual Environment. *Journal of Science Education and Technology*, 16(1), 99–111.

Kirriemuir, J. & McFarlan, A. (2004). *Literature review in games and learning.* Bristol: FutureLab series.

Lauwaert, M. (2007). Challenge Everything? : Construction Play in Will Wright's SIMCITY. *Games and Culture,* 2(3), 194–212.

Lim, C. P.; Nonis, D. & Hedberg, J. (2006). Gaming in a 3D Multiuser Virtual Environment: Engaging Students in Science Lesson. *British Journal of Educational Technology,* 37(2), 211–231.

Linderoth, J. (2004). *Datorspelandets mening : bortom idén om den interaktiva illusionen.* Doctoral thesis. Göteborg: Acta Universitatis Gothoburgensis.

Ljung-Djärf, A. (2004). *Spelet runt datorn : Datoranvändande som meningsskapande praktik i förskolan.* Doctoral thesis. Malmö: Malmö University.

Lyons, T. (2006). Different Countries, Same Science Classes: Students' experience of school science classes in their own words. *International Journal of Science Education*, 28(6), 591-613.

Magnussen, R. (2008): *Representational Inquiry in Science Learning Games.* Doctoral thesis. Copenhagen: Danish School of Education, University of Aarhus.

Malone, T. (1981). *What makes things fun to learn? A study of instrinsically motivating computer games.* Palo Alto, CA: Xerox.

Mathevet, R. ; Le Page, C. ; Etienne, M. ; Lefebvre, G. ; Poulin, B. & Gigot, G. (2007). BUTORSTAR: A role-playing game for collective awareness of wise reedbed use. *Simulation Gaming,* 38(2), 233–262.

Maxis (2003). *SimCity 4 Deluxe Edition.* Redwood City, CA: Electronic Arts.

Nilsson, E. M. & Jakobsson, A. (Submitted). Simulated sustainable societies: students' reflections on creating future cities in computer games. *Manuscript submitted.*

Nelson, B.; Ketelhut, D. J.; Clarke, J.; Bowman, C. & Dede, C. (2005). Design-based research strategies for developing a scientific inquiry curriculum in a multi-user virtual environment. *Educational Technology,* 45(1), 21–34.

Neulight, N.; Kafai, Y. B.; Kao, L.; Foley, B. & Galas, C. (2007). Children's participation in a Virtual Epidemic in the Science Classroom: Making connection to Natural Infectious Disease. *Journal of Science Education and Technology,* 16(1), 47–58.

OECD (2003). *The PISA 2003 Assessment Framework.* Paris: Organisation for Economic Co Operation and Development.

O'Connor, J. (1997). *The art of systems thinking : essential skills for creativity and problem solving*. London: Thorsons.

Price, C. B. (2008). Learning Physics with the Unreal Tournament Engine. *Physics Education,* 43(3), 291–337.

Rehn, A.; Persson, S. & Svingby, G. (2007). *Lasarus. Utprövning av ett datorspel om människokroppen, hälsa och sjukvård på elever i skolår 3–7. (Lazarus. A computer game on the body, health and care tested on students aged 10–14).* Malmö: Malmö University.

Rieber, L. P. & Noah, D. (2008). Games, Simulations, and Visual Metaphors in Education: Antagonism between Enjoyment and Learning. *Educational Media International*, 45(2), 77–92.

Salen, K. (2008). *The ecology of games : connecting youth, games, and learning*. Cambridge, MA: MIT Press.

Sandford, R.; Ulicsak, M.; Facer, K. & Rudd, T. (2006). *Teaching with Games Using commercial off-the-shelf computer games in formal education.* Bristol: FutureLab series.

Sim, G.; MacFarlane, S. & Read, J. (2006). All work and no play: Measuring fun, usability, and learning in software for children. *Computers & Education*, 46, 235–248.

Squire, K. & Jan, M. (2007). Mad City Mystery: Developing Scientific Argumentation Skills with a Place-based Augmented Reality Game on Handheld Computer. *Journal of Science Education and Technology,* 16(1), 5–29.

Squire, K. & Klopfer, E. (2007). Augmented Reality Simulations on Handheld Computers. *Journal of the Learning Sciences,* 16(3), 371–413.

Svingby, G. & Nilsson, E. M. (In progress). Research review: empirical studies on computer gameplay in the science classroom. *To be submitted.*

Swedish Media Council (2008). *Ungar & medier 2008*. Stockholm: Ministry of Education, Research and Culture, Swedish Government.

The Swedish National Agency for Education (2009). IT-användning och IT-kompetens : Redovisning av uppdrag om uppföljning av IT-användning och IT-kompetens i förskola, skola och vuxenutbildning. Stockholm: Skolverket. www.skolverket.se/publikationer?id=2192

Van Eck, R. (2006). Digital Game-Based Learning: It's Not Just the Digital Natives Who Are Restless. *EDUCAUSE Review,* 41(2), 16–30.

In: Interactive and Digital Media for Education in Virtual … ISBN: 978-1-61668-844-8
Editor: Cai Yiyu

Chapter 3

Deconstructing Learning Games as Fun, Educative and Realistic

Thomas Duus Henriksen
The Danish School of Education, University of Aarhus, Denmark

Abstract

This chapter explores the notions of thinking on learning games as something fun, based on content exploration, and as realistic. By exploring a learning game on change management, the chapter attempts to disconnect from those solutions to the problems on how to incite participation in learning games, how to create its learning processes and how to understand the quality of the experience. By unsettling the commonly accepted answers to those questions, alternative opportunities and their effects are explored in order to provide opportunities for innovating the use and design of learning games by rethinking the didactic design for using such games to facilitate learning processes.

Introduction: Approaching the Foundation of Learning Games

While the purpose of a game is to provide its player with immersive experiences, the purpose of a learning game is to extend itself into the lived lives of the participants. To do so, game-designers draw upon experiences from commercial gaming, using fun to create immersive experiences while exploring an academically enriched content, and doing so under the assumption that the knowledge of the game will be transferable to game-external situations.

In the current chapter, the widely accepted approach of thinking of learning games as something fun, based on the exploration of a realistic, educative content is explored while questioned whether it is the most appropriate basis for creating learning processes through games. To do so, an adult learning game called the EIS Simulation is explored in order to find alternative approaches for thinking games into learning, which can be applied to designing VLE for other target groups.

The analytical approach of this chapter follows Gilles Deleuze's (1994) attention to the relationship between problems and solutions, as expressed through his concepts of actual and virtual. According to Deleuze, Western philosophy has had a tendency to emphasize the actual solution through an emphasis on solving problems and defining phenomenon. Instead, he proposes a shift of attention away from the currently actualized solution, and towards the underlying problem. Rather than trying to define how one should live or how one should think of games, Deleuzian philosophy would ask the question on how one might think of games, thereby allowing the virtual, or alternative solutions, to be assessed. The key purpose is to disconnect from the rationality that privileges learning games in some particular manner, in this case as fun, educative and realistic, and instead try to assess those underlying questions that they are solutions to. A key point here is to consider the current as being merely one among several possible solutions, to address the rationalities that privilege the current as the solution to how one should think of learning games, and in particular, not to consider alternatives in contrast to the actual, but in regard to the underlying problem that they are trying to provide a solution to. The whole effort is an attempt to liquidate the current understandings of learning games in order to provide manners of innovating learning games beyond thinking development as more fun, more content and more realism.

The question is then, what are the dominating answers then answers to; by making learning games fun, by making them educative through an exploration of an academically enriched content, and as realistic representations of an issue? By mobilizing the discourse analysis found with Laclau & Mouffe (1985), the answers can be understood as those discourses that have managed to dominate the nodal points of learning games, and by that provide its key issues with a particular meaning. Nodal points are distinct as their occupant not only provide the nodal point with meaning, but allows its surrounding elements to become colored by the occupant's meaning as well. If, for example, the nodal of game experience were to be occupied by a realistic discourse, it would state that the participant's experience should be sensation of realism, a meaning that would spread to surrounding issues like graphics, game-mechanics and sound. By occupying a nodal point, a discourse provides the whole with a particular understanding, rendering alternative understandings as invalid, thereby closing the issue. Anyone suggesting something different than the reigning discourse is by definition wrong. The reason for addressing the issues of fun, educative content and realism is to address those discourses that have not been actualized as dominating, and by them reopening the issue on how to think, use and design learning games.

It is not always easy to address such ex-courses, as the dominating discourses are often deployed in a very powerful manner. This can be seen while challenging the idea that learning games should be fun, which is often met by a Derridan question like "Should they rather be boring?", thereby keeping the current discourse of fun in the office by framing the alternative as absurd. However, according to Deleuze, such comparison would merely be a comparison on the basis of those rationalities that privileged fun as an answer in the first place. To truly explore the innovative options, the underlying problem must be reassessed, and the alternative understood as a possible solution to it. Rather than looking at alternatives to the dominating answers fun, content and realism, the aim of this chapter is to readdress the questions on how to incite participation, how to create a learning process, and how to understand the game-provided experience. Through this shift of emphasis, focus is shifted from the current solutions to virtual problems, and by it an opportunity to explore the diversity of the problem, rather than merely focusing on those perspectives that can be seen through a given solution.

EMPIRICAL FOUNDATION: THE EIS SIMULATION

In order to address the issues of fun, content and realism, the experiences of a French learning game is explored, using it as an example on how alternative understandings can be seen as present in a learning game. The game is briefly introduced and then discussed according to the 3 nodals.

The EIS Simulation (EIS) is a learning game for teaching change management to MBA students and middle managers. It has been developed at the French business university Insead, and is widely used in organizations like IKEA, FIAT and the US Defence. The game presents its participants with a story about a large company called EuroComm which buys a smaller company called TeleSwitches, and then wants the smaller company to start using a specific ITC system – the EIS. Playing the roles of change agents, the participants are sent from the larger company to the smaller with one mission: to persuade the top management of TeleSwitches to adopt the EIS.

To do so, the participants are given access to 18 different change initiatives and 120 game-days. The game is then played by investing game-days into those different initiatives, and through those initiatives persuading the 24 members of the top management. An example would be to invest 3 days in asking the editor of the internal magazine to include a short article on the benefits of using the EIS, which might create some awareness about the EIS, or to invest 5 days in organizing a workshop for those managers that are already interested.

The aim for the participants is to make all the 24 characters in the game adopt the system, first by making them aware of it, then interested in it, to make them try it, and then finally adopt it. Scores are measured by counting the number of adopters, as well as measuring the combined support of those 24 characters. The game is played in groups of 4-5, and a game typically runs for 100-120 minutes, involving some 30-50 decisions. The game is extremely difficult, and average scores are about 30% of the possible, achievable score. After the game, participants are debriefed and their experiences are discussed. In this chapter, two deployments of the EIS are referred to; the XX, which ran as an open course, and the YY, which ran as an internal company course.

ADDRESSING THE NODALS

In order to address the issues of fun, content and realism, the three nodal occupations are discussed on basis of the current literature on learning games. Experiences from the EIS are then used for addressing those discourses that are made invisible by the dominating discourse.

Nodal 1: Fun and the Participatory Incentive

Needless to say, making games fun is the key objective when it comes to commercial gaming. Game-design literature is rich on perspectives on how to put fun into games (see Bates, 2001; Rouse, 2001), to avoid fun-killers (see Fullerton *et al.*, 2004), or balancing fun against issues like realism (see Bates, 2001). The purpose of these efforts is to create enjoyable experiences that motivate the player, and what educational designer has not been astonished by the immersion of players into games like 'World of Warcraft' and wondered how such motivation could be harnessed for learning purposes? Such conjunction of learning and playing is seen within edutainment, a special breed of games used for educational purposes (see Konzack, 2003). Although a moderately successful industry, it has been criticized for falling between two chairs (see Egenfeldt-Nielsen, 2005), either by making weak learning processes, or by failing to make good games. Despite such challenges, Prensky (2001) considers this conjunction to be the purpose of learning games. Compared to commercial gaming, such games are often a compromise, as described by Bates:

"In the end, fun game play is more important than realism, so if a balance can't be found and a tradeoff is necessary, fun wins" (Bates, 2004, p. 65).

This gives commercial game designers more freedom to meet what experience the player would appreciate the most, whereas the balancing represents a key issue to educational game designers. The area has, despite, maintained its emphasis on fun as a heritage from commercial gaming, as well as the understanding of games it came with. Within learning games, fun is given the same position as in commercial gaming, seeking to make learning fun (see Barab *et al.*, 2001) in order to motivate participation.

When Challenging Fun as The Participatory Incentive

In terms of discourse analysis, the answer fun has clearly managed to occupy the issue of motivation. This heritage is largely unchallenged, and while being fun is the prime purpose of a commercial game, the same understanding is handed down to learning games, where they are often seen as a means for bringing fun into the educational setting. Learning games are often presented to participants as something fun to look forward to, and among participants, the expectation of the participation in a learning game is often shaped to this understanding. It is so deeply embedded that it is beyond question, and by eliminating the contingency, a shared understanding is manifested. This becomes very clear when the discourse is challenged, which often results in framing the logical opposite as both unattractive and absurd.

By allowing the question of motivation to be answered by the fun discourse, fun becomes the key driver for the process, as well as to the whole question on why to use learning games. When a discourse is allowed to dominate the question proposed in a nodal, in this case the question on participational incentives in learning games, the effect has two faces:

1) it provides the right answer, in this case stating that learning games should be fun in order to motivate the participant into taking part in the activity (which is then assumed to be educative).
2) while constituting one understanding as right, it renders alternative understandings as being wrong, in this case proposing the purpose of learning games to be something different than being fun. Question is what opportunities those wrong answers can provide in terms of inciting participation.

One approach would be to elaborate on the conception of fun while asking what alternative understandings might exist within the current terminology. One radical suggestion is proposed by Papert's (1998) concept of hard fun as the result of frustration and challenge. A more radical approach would be to investigate what alternatives would go beyond the current understanding of the purpose: rather than seeing the game as a tool for motivation, emphasis can be moved to seeing it as an educational tool. Instead of asking how a specific learning process can be made fun (through a learning game), it is relevant to ask how to incite participation in a specific learning process, and by it to move emphasis away from fun as an answer (discourse), to the question of inciting participation (nodal), thereby opening the issue to competing discourses. One such approach is provided by Lepper & Malone's (1985) framework for creating motivation in learning processes, emphasizing feedback as the most significant determinant in creating intrinsic motivation, comprising challenge, curiosity, control, fantasy and interpersonal incentives as tools for enhancing the effect of extrinsic incentives. The aim of using their analytical attention would be to point out that although fun would be the dominating discourse on the question of why learning games, it is important to see how other discourses are active and affect the field in order to be able to innovate on the area.

THE PARTICIPATORY INCENTIVES OF THE EIS

When studying the participatory incentives involved in playing the EIS, fun can be recognised in the tone of the game's feedback and in the presentation of the game, but is far from being a dominant participatory incentive. Instead, the EIS provides an untraditional approach to producing participatory incentives, and while the game is originally presented to the participants as a fun experience to take part of, other participational incentives are active in the persuasion of the participant into taking part of the game, and most importantly, to remain a part throughout the game.

Mobilising a Sense of Urgency on a Subject

Using Lepper & Malone's diversity of incentives, the participatory incentive can be seen as a socially constituted desire to display control of the game. During a deployment of the EIS, the subject of the game, change, is presented as something important, but also as something difficult for organizations to handle. Hence the participants being middle managers or MBA students, change competency can be seen as an attractive competence to master, and as the game is presented as an opportunity to display change competency, the game becomes desirable for the participants to play and to control. Performing well in the game is thereby constructed as a ticket into the attractive club of those able to handle change and vice versa.

The social constitution of participatory incentives provides a profound persistence among participants to keep playing the game. As mentioned earlier, participants playing the game are likely to score about 30% of the possible score, which is less than they desire. As the participants play the game, they gradually realize that they will not earn the desired bragging-rights of having won the game, but despite the frustration, they remain in the game. Rather than giving up, they give it a try, well knowing that they had engaged themselves in a problem that was much harder than they are skilled for. While trying to make the best of it, they tried to crack its underlying mechanics to get at least some of the game's highly desired points, and by them, avoiding to lose face to other participants.

Allowing it to be Harder than it Looks

A key consequence of the staged participatory incentive is that it produced a participatory persistence, even when the game got harder than it seemed, making the fun discourse barely visible, being less dominant to the game. This goes against the notion of flow (Csikszentmihalyi, 1975), which is commonly accepted by game-designers as the recipe for creating game-experiences highly motivating, namely by constantly matching the game-challenge with the participants' abilities. By instead staging game-mastery of the EIS as desirable, the participants engage themselves persistently in a hard problem, while trying to reach the desirable position of mastering it by developing the proper skills for it. Every time the participants master a problem, the game provides a token of mastery (in terms of points), for then to stage a new, difficult problem to the participant. Due to the participant's acceptance of the task as desirable, the participant accepts the frustration of the challenge. This transition between staging, conveyance, solving and mastering is illustrated below.

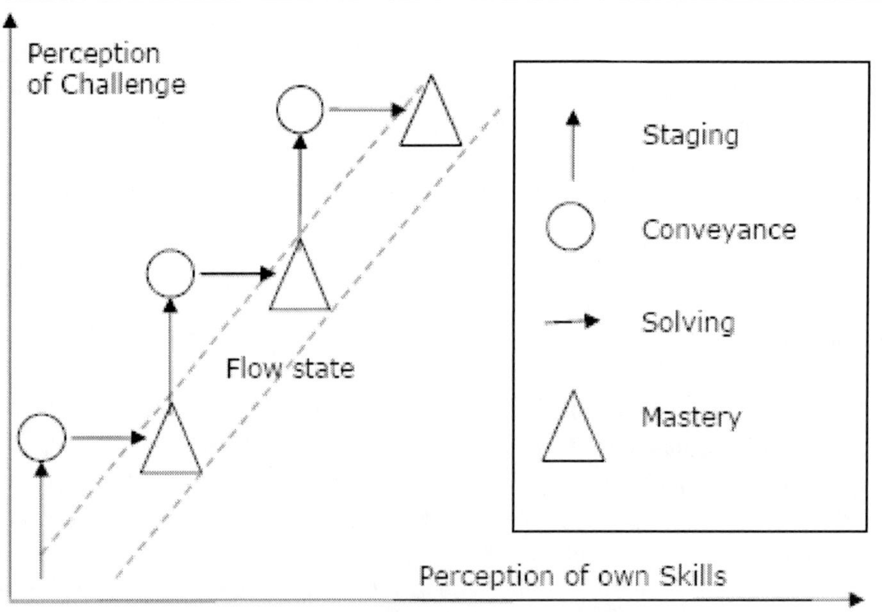

Figure 1. Staging vs. flow (originally presented with Henriksen, 2006b).

From this conception, it would seem that a frustration-based incentive is less sensitive to differences in individual participant skills than that of a flow-based, allowing a larger discrepancy between the game level and the participant skill. Such a staging of the socially desirable is able to draw upon game-external sources for motivating behavior, allowing the designer to use a wider array of tools for constituting engagement in learning games, rather than trying to make the game fun. This does not mean that the game has to be boring (or preclude the use of fun), but that the game-designer must readdress the underlying problem of inciting participation, and use the participatory incentive must suitable to the desired process of participation.

Nodal 2: Educative Content and the Learning Process

Having addressed fun as a dominating discourse for the participatory incentive, the next question becomes 'participating in what', thereby addressing the learning process of the learning game. When deploying fun as the participatory incentive, Bates (2004) pointed at the act of prioritizing between fun and realism, which for learning games would be a question of balancing between fun and an academically enriched content that would represent whatever was to be learned though the game. From this perspective, the learning game-designer's job would then be to turn some academic knowledge into mechanics and stories for the participant to explore and theories on game based learning would address how such processes were designed, as well as how the participant would benefit from them. This line of thinking is found with Shaffer & Resnick (1999), who argues for the provision of authenticity in learning experiences, allowing learners to investigate complex systems, as well as with Aldrich (2004) who emphasizes the role of the content in the educational experience. However, like in a game of Jeopardy, content is merely an answer, the interesting part would be the question leading to it. Content is merely an actualization of an underlying problem, from which alternative intensities can be explored and other virtual solutions can become actualized. Here, the underlying problem is how to create learning processes through games, making it relevant to address what rationalities hold the two together. An example of such rationality can be found in Malone & Lepper's (1987) concept of endogenous game-design, which tries to draw a straight line between the dynamics of the phenomenon or subject taught, and the game-mechanics that attempt to represent it. The philosophy of learning underlying such an approach would resemble the practice-oriented thinking found with Lave (1999), which assumes that the participatory exploration of a phenomenon or practice is likely to produce learning processes. This approach has been conceptualized as a game's ability to produce explorable, simulated practices (Henriksen, 2000, 2002), which can provide the participant with practical conceptions of such. From such lines of thinking, it is not surprising that the answer on how participants learn from learning games becomes by exploring an academically enriched content, as with the Derridan question of fun, it would make little sense to claim that the content should not be related to the academic subject. The underlying discourse of content is commonly enacted during design or game presentations through utterances addressing what to put into the game, what the game does or what you can learn from the game. By being able to explicitly embed an academic content into a game that game gains a unique selling point; while being comparable in content to other educational initiatives, emphasis can be turned towards other qualities like its ability to incite participation or provide feedback on specific decisions.

By allowing the content discourse to occupy the question of learning, the game process becomes a question of exploring the embedded content, and in the end, to master its information and dynamics. As with most e-learning, this process of exploration becomes synonymous with learning, allowing the designer to focus on optimizing this explorative process. The heritage of the content discourse points back to traditional commercial game-design, which emphasizes the game as something that starts when it starts and ends when it ends. It also employs a very rational approach to learning, assuming learning to take place upon exposure to knowledge. In order to meet with processual shortcomings, a facilitator can be deployed in order to repeat the game's points, and eventually de-contextualize them into theoretical concepts (see Henriksen, 2004). Although such activities attempt to expand the learning process beyond the time span of the game, focus has remained on designing and exploring content. The content discourse has two key consequences:

1) it provides a clear answer on where to embed or look for the educational benefit in learning games, in this case in the content
2) it states that if it is not in the content, it is missing.

This has a clear impact on the underlying model of learning, which would state that the participant is able and expected to learn the content of the learning game, as well as relying heavily on a realistic, practice orientated approach to learning. While such shared understanding provides consensus on how to put learning into games it becomes relevant to challenge its fixation in order to innovate learning games. This can be done by displacing focus away from content, thereby allowing alternative discourses to be seen. In regard to the EIS, four analytical displacements can be seen in the cracks in the current discourse: time, objective, orientation and nature of the knowledge, which are addressed below:

Time and Learning

When designing a course or a seminar, the first thing one is short on is time. Consequently, learning games are often deployed in respect to how long the actual game takes and less attention is paid to the preceding and following activities. Such prioritizing can be seen as a direct consequence of the content discourse, to which pre- and post activities merely are seen as supportive, whereas the game holds the real learning experience. The two deployments of the EIS studied provide different views on learning game deployment. While the introduction to the game was very alike between the two sessions, the game-facilitation and the post activities differed. In respect to the pre-activities, they consisted of two elements:

1) a general introduction to the subject taught (change).
2) an introduction to the game, consisting of
    a) a narrative introduction to the game's story,
    b) a ludological introduction on how to navigate the game mechanics and play the game,
    c) an introduction to the game interface.

In respect to the game-facilitation, the first (XX) deployment employed a 1-2-1 deployment (see Henriksen, 2004), starting with a theoretical approach to change, then the game was deployed as a practical approach, and then it returned to a theoretical approach via the debriefing. The second (YY) deployment utilized a theoretically informed approach (TiA), through which the game was played in thirds, interrupted by theory sessions on relevant issues. Score and process for the different groups were concluded after the game, and then its challenges. With the XX deployment, the key issues were addressed, and the game discussed, whereas the YY group discussed the game in respect to external problems, followed by workshops on how to use the insights from the game.

Both deployments placed a significant element of learning activities outside the game, allowing the two to have a mutually supportive function. Whereas the introduction sought to equip the participants theoretically to meet the challenge, the game provided an opportunity for seeing some of the introduced perspectives in practice, which again worked as a practical example or experience for the post-activities and its theories. As TiA approach provided an interrupting experience to the participants' game-flow, the connection between theoretical perspectives was strengthened. This time perspective allows the learning processes to be seen as encompassing both theoretical introductions and follow-ups, and as relations between theory and the game activity.

Objective to Learn

When thinking in lines of content, the learning objective would logically be to communicate as much of its content from the learning game to the participant by maximizing the exposure to it. But rather than seeing success in line with having communicated content, it would be relevant to see what other objectives the learning game would be able to stage processes from. Such emphasis employs Højbjerg's (2005) distinction between decisional and negotiational game-processes, from which the EIS can be seen as a game of making the right decision (in respect to content), or to negotiate what decision to make (derived from content), or their combinations. Through such analytical perspective, attention is paid to how the decisions and operations concerning content allow the staging of other (derived) processes. The first would be the group process encountered at the XX deployment, the second the applicative discussion encountered with the YY deployment.

Staged Group Processes

At the XX deployment, disagreements among the participants on what decisions to make turned the group process in an unexpected direction. In terms of exploring content, it turned out problematic by inhibiting the exploration, but in respect to thinking in different learning objectives, the game managed to stage a group process in respect to cooperation concerning cultural and educational differences, risk willingness, and planning. Although diverting from the intended content, it produced a sound experience on handling differences in a conflictual situation. This process derived from the game content, but draws extensively on the setup of the learning game. It also allowed for an open-ended process; while there are rights and wrongs to be explored from the game content, the staged processes would address the social constructions taking place among the participants. In terms of learning objectives, learning games provide an opportunity to stage learning processes that are not directly associated with the communication of an embedded content; rather they can be understood as constituted by it.

ORIENTATION OF ATTENTION

When thinking in lines of content, a connection is assumed between the explored content and real-world issues, thereby creating a need for addressing what is actually being explored. When looking into the two EIS deployments, their orientations diverge: in the XX deployment, attention was staged towards the game as an understanding of change. This was supported by generic examples on how to explain the processes and feedback of the game. In contrast, the YY deployment was staged towards exploring how the participants could understand their organizational realities on the basis of the game. This difference indicates the orientations of the two sessions; the XX sought to understand the game, while the YY sought to provide its participants with analytical tools for understanding, planning and implementing future change projects. While the XX was turned inwards, the YY was turned outwards.

Nature of the Knowledge to be Learned

The content discourse not only affects the learning process, it also determines how and what kinds of knowledge are being learned. When thinking in lines of content, the learning process becomes what Sfard (1998) would describe as acquisitional in the attempt to transfer knowledge from the game to the participant. Such an acquisitional process would encourage the participant to experience and remember as much possible of the content while accommodating the understandings it proposes, but Sfard's point is to warn against trying to understand learning through one lens, proposing that to grasp a fuller picture, it must be understood as both acquisitional and participatory.

This difference can be seen across the two deployments of the EIS. The XX deployment sought to produce an acquisitional process by letting the participants continuously formulate hypotheses of cause and effect while trying to acquire the game-embedded understanding. The YY deployment sought to produce a more participatory approach while allowing the participants to reflect the claims made by the game, using them as analytical perspectives for creating an understanding for their own organization. This allowed the participants to socially construct local understandings on the subject, thereby breaking with the knowledge-monopoly that the game would have from the content perspective. When breaking with the idea of understanding the learning process on basis of content exploration, other didactic activities like reflection, de-contextualization, theory introduction and analysis, as well as re-contextualization become legitimate replacements for the explore-acquisition-transfer approach.

From Learning Games to Game-Based Learning

In respect to time, objective, orientation and the nature of knowledge in learning games, the EIS provided four alternative discourses for understanding, deploying and developing learning games; rather than understanding the learning process as limited to the time spent playing the game, learning processes can be pursued in relation to colonialising before and after activities, while de-emphasising the duration itself; rather than exploring the communication of an academic content, objectives can be looked for as derived activities, both in respect to time and subject; rather than understanding the purpose of the learning session as oriented towards the game activity, the learning process can address issues that are external to the activity in terms of succeeding practices; and rather than thinking of the educational benefit in terms of representative knowledge, it can be thought of as the construction of new knowledge. The key idea is not to see the different processes as replacive, but as design-dimensions (Henriksen, 2006a), as tools for creating learning processes that comply with the educational objective beyond mere knowledge acquisition. While the content-approach offers a straight-forward approach, it is important to notice its shortcomings in terms of producing the diversity of learning processes that are needed to comply with different learning objectives. With emphasis placed on learning games, the game design would be crucial, but with the change of emphasis towards game-based learning, the didactical design of the interplay between the game and the surrounding activities becomes the new key issue to address, which calls for a more inclusive understanding of learning games.

Nodal 3: Realistic Representation and the Experience Validation

The third discourse challenged in this chapter is the idea of games as representational realism, and how it affects our understanding of learning games. As with all discourse analysis, seeing an issue as irrelevant to pursue is an indication of the power of that particular discourse, and when it comes to realism, not seeing a need for addressing the issue is a clear indication of dominance. Like with the previous nodals, the question of the quality of the experience has a powerful impact on the surrounding issues, but this one also has a key influence on the two previous nodals as it concerns how the game is to be understood as a whole. The mobilization of realism provides the game-based experience with a representational value, allowing it to be seen and used as e.g. a practical experience on a subject, thereby making it a valid source to learn from. As a facilitator puts it to his participants:

> "It's frustrating, I can tell you now that it is not an easy game. But at the same time, it's a game that resembles very much the reality that many managers have to face in their organizations."

Here, realism is mobilized through a resemblance to reality, thereby making it believable to the participants, thereby creating the assumption that if the participant is able to handle (and eventually win) the game, that participant will be able to handle similar challenges outside the game. This mobilization provides a clear answer to how to understand the knowledge and insights presented by the learning game, thereby allowing its content and mechanics to be understood as representative, allowing the experience to be used as the basis for practice exploration (Lave, 1999), simulated practice learning (Henriksen, 2000), or Dewey´s (1938) concept of learning by doing. Such theories both allow us to understand the learning process, as well as imbuing the game with legitimacy as an educational tool, thereby opening the gates for the content and fun discourses.

Although seeing the experience produced by the learning games as realistic might seem pretty obvious, this answer to how the game would be experienced from a Deleuzian perspective would merely be one actualization of some intensities of the underlying problem on how to understand the qualities of the experience. From this post-structuralist perspective, realism is merely a powerful construction that states the game to be believable, but according to Henriksen (2006c), a game is merely a representation of a theory, which again is a representation of a phenomenon. The game then becomes an interpretation of an interpretation, turning the game into a perspective on the underlying problem, making it relevant to address how such a sensation of realism is established and maintained.

Facilitator's Call to Reality

Realism is often constituted by making calls to real-world resemblance, and by it, establishing believability. As such a position is achieved (rather than given), it must be taken and defended, a negotiation that becomes clearly visible when the discursive defenses are provoked. As one facilitator puts it

> "[W]hich alternative do you have apart [from] presenting the game as being realistic, given that it is based on insights from reality? Would you introduce the session by saying [:] This game is NOT realistic [?]. "

Such a statement is clearly an attempt to defend the manner that the particular game is to be experienced, and what qualities are to be associated with them. From a realist perspective, the game-designer's experience of some phenomenon is likely to be understood as representative, as can theories on the subject be understood, but from a constructivist perspective, such an approach would merely blind the participant from the perspective that the game was based upon. Objectivity thereby becomes a matter of disconnecting a result from its becoming, which is another approach to establishing a sensation of realism.

When Participants Make Calls to Reality

Another approach to establishing realism is by obscuring the becoming of a result, which in a learning game would mean that the participant was presented with a result, but without the means for understanding how that result came to apply. In the same manner that realism is constructed by facilitators and game-designers, do participants attempt to unsettle it by calling foul play:

> "That's not realistic!" followed by utterances such as "That would never happen to me" or "This would never be the case at YY – we don't even have such gatekeepers.".

Realism becomes a matter of agreeing or not with the result, and if addressed within the realistic discourse, there is only room for one reality, and the other has to be turned down. This is a key consequence of thinking of learning games as realistic; the participants would either become duped with the understandings of the game, or dismiss it as a whole. However, such conflict is not to be resolved in an either-or fashion, instead it provides the facilitator with an opportunity to explore the realities of the participants on the basis of the ideas found in the game. Rather than stating that the game is right, the conflict can be used to explore how the phenomenon, its mechanics or its effects can be seen in the realities of the participants, eventually resulting in an image that is different from that proposed by the game. A key question lies in whether the aim of the game is to learn the game or to explore some game-external reality. The game-provided perspectives can then be used for asking what would happen in reality, what precautions would prevent certain things from happening, or how something could be understood in respect to the gatekeeper function. Through this perspective, the game is seen as experience, based on certain game-embedded, theoretical perspectives, which are usable for understanding certain phenomenon.

Reality and the Focused Perspective

A different approach to constituting reality is through increased complexity, either by increasing the number of interacting factors, often to a degree that makes the game too complicated to grasp, or by obscuring those factors by hiding them in the game-mechanics. Such a maneuver is often made in order to preempt criticism that would point towards areas within the subject that would have been relevant to include, which is a commonly encountered criticism within the field of learning games. From the realist perspective, by stating that something essential is missing, this would challenge the game's ability to fully represent the subject, thereby making it possible to invalidate it. Instead, the post-structuralist perspective would abandon the whole idea of game-representativeness, and instead allow it to be understood as a particular perspective, which would have to be complimented by others. From this perspective, the EIS would become a game on how to communicate change implementation, rather than covering the full spectrum of organizational change.

In addition, the participants' statements on why a game was not realistic would allow an exploration of those rationalities that bound together particular understandings with particular experiences. By addressing the statement, "This would never be the case at YY-company – we don't even have such gatekeepers" would raise questions like, "did the participant fail to notice some taken for granted process or relation in his or her own organization, has the participant ever been subjected to the phenomenon discussed, or is the participant simply right?" By liquidating the perspective privileged by realism, the conclusions of the game can be liquidated as such, thereby turning them into analytical perspectives for understanding game-external events. Through this approach, the game-provided perspectives become valid, not as something in themselves, but in the situation they are applied, and by it, to address the effects of those phenomena.

Rather than trying to privilege the knowledge and experiences of the game as representational, thinking of learning games as a means for embracing discrepancies holds an opportunity for using those to analyze the different rationalities that bind together understanding and experience. Such learning processes become available when abandoning the idea that the alternative to realism is fiction, but instead attempts to focus on the underlying problem of how to understand the experience produced by learning games.

CONCLUSION: FROM EDUTAINING TO STAGING

The key point of this chapter has been to explore the opportunities that become available when starting to see the current conceptions of learning games as something fun, based on content exploration and as something realistic as mere actualizations of the underlying problems of inciting participation, creating learning processes and understanding the game-provided experience. By returning to those underlying problems, focus could be shifted towards an exploration of the virtual alternatives, and in particular those rationalities, which bound together an understanding of a problem and a solution that privileged some particular understandings over others.

Using the EIS as case-example, focus was turned towards understanding how participatory incentives were established, rather than inherent to the game-form, how learning processes could take place through a didactic interplay between a range of activities, rather than being a mere exploration and acceptance of the game's content, and how to use the perspectives and their becoming as analytical scopes, rather than being duped with the understanding of the game as realistic. By returning to the problems underlying these discussions, whole new opportunities lie available for innovating the use and design of learning games. At some point, it might take some of the game-element out of learning games, but that might just be the key to take them to the next level of effectiveness.

AUTHOR INFO

Dr Duus Henriksen is with The Danish School of Education, University of Aarhus, Denmark. He uses a diversity of learning games in his research in order to explore the relationship between emotions and learning. Besides his research, Thomas acts as a project consultant on projects within the area of learning games, supervises psychology students within the area of industrial/organisational psychology, as well as supervises diverse internal and external projects concerning learning games and game design. Besides working at Learning Lab Denmark and the Danish University of Education, Thomas works as a business psychologist, specialising in game-based learning. He has designed learning games within the areas of organisational development, leadership, management, diverse business economical problems, project management, negotiation, as well as the area of psychological work environments.

Dr Duus Henriksen
The Danish School of Education, University of Aarhus, Denmark
Phone: +45 31215154
Email: tdh@dpu.dk

REFERENCES

Aldrich, C. (2004). *Simulations and the future of learning: An innovative (and perhaps revolutionary) approach to e-learning. San Francisco*: John Wiley & Sons, Inc.

Barab, S. A., Hay, K. E., Barnett, M., & Squire, K. (2001). Constructing virtual worlds: Tracing the historical development of learner practices. *Cognition and instruction*, 19(1), 47.

Bates, B. (2001). *Game design: The art & business of creating games*: Prima Publishing.

Bates, B. (2004). *Game design* (2.nd ed.): Prima Publishing.

Csikszentmihalyi, M. (1975). *Flow*. The psychology of optimal experience. New York: Harper & Row.

Deleuze, G. (1994). *Difference and repetition* (P. Patton, Trans.). London: The Athlone Press.

Dewey, J. (1938). Experience and education. *In J. A. Boydston* (Ed.), Later works 13: S. Illnois University Press.

Egenfeldt-Nielsen, S. (2005). *Beyond edutainment: Exploring the educational potential of computer games*. ITU, København.

Fullerton, T., Swain, C., & Hoffman, S. (2004). *Game design workshop: Designing, prototyping, and playtesting games*. San Francisco: CMP Books.

Henriksen, T. D. (2000). *Læring i den simulerede praksis*. Københavns Universitet, Københahavn.

Henriksen, T. D. (2002). Hvordan kan man lære gennem fiction? Teoretiske perspektiver på læring gennem deltagelse i rollespilsformidlet fiktion (how can we learn through fiction? *Theoretical perspectives on learning through participation in role-play based fiction).* University of Copenhagen.

Henriksen, T. D. (2004). On the transmutation of educational role-play: A critical reframing to the role-play in order to meet the educational demands. In M. Montola & J. Stenros (Eds.), *Beyond role and play. Tools, toys and theory for harnessing the imagination* (pp. 107-130). Helsinki, FI: Ropecon ry.

Henriksen, T. D. (2006a). *Dimensions in educational game-design. Perspectives on designing and implementing game-based learning processes in the educational setting.,* Evrópumiðstöð. Reykjavik, Iceland.

Henriksen, T. D. (2006b). Educational role-play: Moving beyond entertainment: Seeking to please or aiming for the stars, *On Playing Roles* (pp. 23). Tampere, Finland.

Henriksen, T. D. (2006c). Games and creativity learning. In T. Fritzon & T. Wrigstad (Eds.), *Role, play, art. Collected experiences of role-playing.* Published in conjunction with the 10th knutpunkt convention (pp. 3-16). Stockholm.

Højbjerg, E. (2005). Spil- og spilleregler - om analytik i samfundsvidenskaben. In A. Esmark, C. B. Lausten & N. Åkerstrøm Andersen (Eds.), *Socialkonstruktivistiske analysestrategier: Roskilde Universitetsforlag.*

Konzack, L. (2003). *Edutainment.*

Laclau, E., & Mouffe, C. (1985). *Hegemony & socialist strategy. Towards a radical democratic politics.* London, New York: Verso.

Lave, J. (1999). Læring, mesterlære, social praksis. In K. Nielsen & S. Kvale (Eds.), *Mesterlære. Læring som social praksis* (pp. 35-53). København: Hans Reitzels Forlag.

Lepper, M. R., & Chabay, R. W. (1985). Intrinsic motivation and instruction: Conflicting views on the role of motivational processes in computer-based education. *Educational Psychologist,* 20(4), 217-230.

Malone, T. W., & Lepper, M. R. (1987). Making leaning fun. A taxonomy of intrinsic motivations for learning. *In Aptitude, learning and instruction* (Vol. Volume 3: Conative and Affective Process Analyses). NJ: Lawrence Erlbaum Associates, Inc. Publishers.

Papert, S. (1998). *Does easy do it? Children, games and learning*. Game Developer(June 1998), 87-88.

Prensky, M. (2001). *Digital game-based learning.*

Rouse, R. (2001). *Game design: Theory & practice.* Plano, Texas: Wordware Publishing, Inc.

Sfard, A. (1998). *On two metaphors for learning and the dangers of choosing just one.* Educational researcher, 27(2), 4.

Shaffer, D. W., & Resnick, M. (1999). "thick" authenticity: New media and authentic learning. *Journal of Interactive Learning Research,* 10(2), 195-215.

In: Interactive and Digital Media for Education in Virtual … ISBN: 978-1-61668-844-8
Editor: Cai Yiyu

Chapter 4

PROCESS MANAGEMENT TOOLS AND LEARNING MANAGEMENT SYSTEMS – A PROACTIVE APPROACH TO E-LEARNING

Karin Tweddell Levinsen
Institute of Curriculum Studies,
Danish School of Education – Aarhus University, Denmark

ABSTRACT

The chapter discusses the slow implementation of LMS in educational organizations. The presented research focuses on Denmark and points at two main courses. The general accepted explanation is that teachers are not competent to exploit the LMS in their everyday work. The author suggests that qualities of current LMS such as adaptability, usability and interaction design may also be considered. It is found that many teachers do in fact need to improve their digital literacy, but it is also found that current LMS produce barriers for digital literate teachers who perform constructivist and social constructivist designs for teaching and learning in virtual environments. These barriers prevent competent teachers from acting as proactive supervisors or coaches, roles which are paramount for performing this kind of student centered pedagogy successfully.

The chapter presents a case study of a Danish blended mode Master Program that demonstrates the consequences of the barriers in relation to learning quality and to fulfilling the learning objectives at the program. The research provides arguments for the provision of Proactive Teaching Tools, which will support the adaptability of LMS and enable the teacher to acquire the necessary awareness of the learning processes and students' progression, during the actual performance of a course. Finally the chapter presents conceptual examples of the functionality of Proactive Teacher Tools.

Keywords: LMS, Proactive Teachers Tools, Process Management, collaborative learning, cooperative learning, online, e-learning.

INTRODUCTION

The transition from the industrial to the networked society challenges the educational system in various ways. The global economy's demand for efficiency and effectiveness calls for increased and sophisticated use of distant, blended and distributed e-learning. The networked and e-permeated society demands students who possess networked society competencies such as self-programming, self-initiated learning and ICT-related literacy. Teachers are expected to conduct their teaching within virtual environments and to support the students' development of networked society competencies. Despite the fact that most teachers belong to the generation called Baby Boomers, Generation X or Matures who have acquired their ICT-competencies as grownups (Dede 2005, Levinsen 2007, Oblinger 2003), they are expected to possess a high level of ICT- literacy that allows them to identify and exploit the opportunities of digitalized learning and teaching environments.

In the industrial pedagogic paradigm (Reigeluth 1999) teachers act as the source of knowledge and perform teacher-centered instructivist teaching and summative product-oriented evaluations that measure the students' ability to perform problem-solving and to reproduce a core curriculum within a formalized and well-defined context. In the networked society, the pedagogic paradigm is constructivist and social constructivist and directed towards future-oriented construction of knowledge (Roberts 2004). The teachers act as supervisors, coaches and knowledge managers, who support and challenge the students' learning process in a student-centered practice with proactive interventions and formative process evaluation methods that measure the students' ability to exploit their gained knowledge within new, weakly defined or unpredictable situations (Yale University 2003, Illeris 2006, Sørensen, Audon & Levinsen forthcoming). The differences can be illuminated by the way learning objects are defined at instructivist and constructivist oriented educations in Denmark respectively (Heilesen & Lerche 2005):

Instructivist	**Constructivist**
The aim of … is to enable you to … The aim is to give you … The course is aimed to enable you to … … concerning answering the assignment	The aim of … is that the students acquire knowledge and take a critical position to … ….students… reflect on and evaluate … The students develop competencies and skills Concerning … reflection on students own practice when applying ….. in concrete cases

In order to meet these demands, teachers have to change their practice from traditional teacher-centered teaching to student-oriented teaching and learning while they simultaneously adapt the student-oriented teaching and learning practice to a virtual environment. The changes and their impact on society have been discussed by governments and international organizations throughout the last decade, and governments and educational institutions all over the world have formulated strategies, launched projects and invested huge sums of money to meet the challenges (European Commission 2003 and 2004, G8 2006, OECD 2001). Despite the strong initiatives and huge investments, the general implementation progress is slow. When it comes to the implementation of LMS (Learning Management Systems) which are the focus of this chapter, they are most frequently used for administrative purposes, document sharing and one-way information rather than used for online or blended mode designs for learning such as CSCL (Computer Supported Collaborative Learning) (Brown, Paewai & Suddaby 2009, Steel 2009).

The slow implementation is also seen in Denmark (Levinsen 2007a) despite an early and huge effort to implement ICT in the educational system and the high level of general digital literacy in the Danish population. Teachers at all levels of the Danish educational system have not yet managed to exploit LMS as drivers in their designs for teaching and learning or in their everyday pedagogical practice. The most frequent conclusion that is drawn due to these results is that the teachers' competencies need to be improved and accordingly most interventions are aiming in that direction. It is obvious that teachers who belong to the so called Baby Boomers, Generation X or Matures and have a acquired computer literacy (Martin 2006) as grownups at a level of basic skills required to perform specific operations, may benefit from in-service training no matter the state of the LMS' usability and interaction design, but what about the ICT competent teachers? The question arises as to what degree the slow implementation is due to the lack of teachers' ICT-related pedagogical competencies and/or due to poor usability and interaction design of the LMS?

The body of literature regarding evaluations of LMS is limited and the majority focuses on technical features or evaluates the efficiency from the students' point of view. Studies from the teachers' point of view of the adaptability of LMS to various designs for teaching and learning and studies of the teachers' working conditions are almost absent (Orngreen & Levinsen 2004/2005, Graf & List 2005, Marko & Honkaranta 2007, Steel 2009). Some researchers discuss that current LMS draw on teacher centered teaching and learning models and therefore influence the teachers acceptance of LMS from a pedagogical point of view (Orngreen &Levinsen 2004/2005, Apedoe 2005; Hedberg 2006; Naidu 2006). The fact is, that we do not know to what extent the problem of slow implementation may be due to the quality of usability and interaction design of the LMS.

In order to explore the role of LMS in the slow implementation, this study focuses on teachers who are both ICT literate and considered innovators and early adopters of ICT in their everyday practice. The present chapter comprises an examination of the work conditions that LMS offer teachers who are experienced users of virtual teaching and learning environments in CSCL online- and blended mode designs for learning. In order to set the stage for discussing LMS viewed as work conditions for these teachers in their everyday educational practice, the following section covers three dimensions: 1) Status of the Danish National Educational Strategy; 2) Empirical studies of the implementation of ICT in Danish educational institutions; and 3) State of the art study of the inherent features of current LMS. Following a context for understanding LMS, the chapter includes a recent case study of actual uses of LMS in a pedagogical practice. The analysis finds a discrepancy between the official aims and goals and the current implementation of ICT in the Danish educational system. It is found that many teachers do not possess the competence to exploit the learning potential of LMS but it is also found, that teachers who do possess the competence and do want to perform designs for teaching and learning that address the national goals and the challenges of the networked society meet severe restrictions and barriers in the usability and interaction design of current LMS. In conclusion the chapter suggests a series of research based improvements for future LMS.

LMS AS WORK CONDITIONS

Status of the Danish National Educational Strategy

Denmark has one of the highest frequencies in the world of PC's and Internet connections in private homes. The government focuses on continuous improvement and development of the populations' access to technology, in private homes, in business, between citizens and public services, as well as in education at all levels (figure 1).

Technology in families:

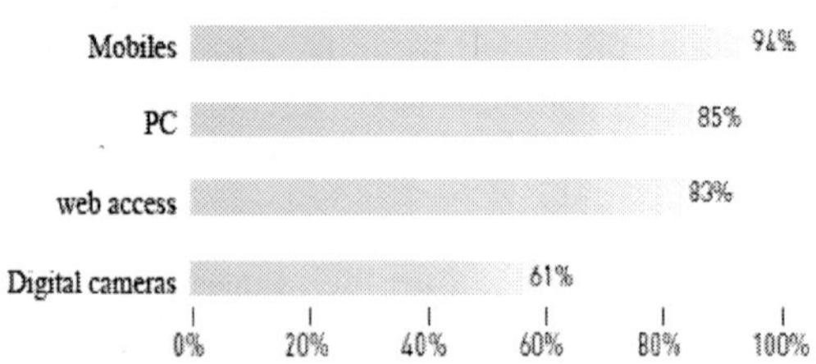

Source: Statistics Denmark 2006

Primary schools:

Five learners pr. PC in 2005.
59% PC's are less that 3 years old
Local wireless and broadband in most schools around 2000

Source: Ministry of Education (Undervisningsministeriet 2007)

Secondary schools:

87% of students and teachers reported their school access to PC's and the web as good

Source: EVA 2005

Figure 1. Danish ICT Statistics (Representations produced by the author).

According to the Danish Ministry of Science, Technology and Innovation (Videnskabsministeriet 2009), it is a precondition for maintenance of the high level of welfare in Denmark that the population possesses the necessary ability of continuous readjustment and lifelong learning in order to deal with future demands in a world of global competition and e-permeation. The Ministry's *National Strategy of ICT-Supported Learning* (Videnska-bsministeriet 2007) rests on strategies defined by OECD and G8. The strategy suggests, among other things, that the educational institutions formulate strategies for digitalisation in terms of networks, the use of LMS and the implementation of ICT-supported learning and e-learning; that ICT literacy is defined with respect to core curriculum, pedagogy and general education; that ICT is integrated in the teacher education; and that all teachers' ICT literacy in general must be strengthened. The relevant networked society competencies for universities, technical colleges, high schools and primary schools are defined by the Ministry of Education in the *National Account for 10 Key Competencies* (Undervisning-sministeriet 2005). The state of these key competencies in the population is regularly measured in order to continuously modify and develop the actual initiatives and interventions. In the case of the universities, the guidelines from the National Educational and ICT Supported Learning Strategies are realized through development contracts with the Danish government. In the case of primary schools, the guidelines are formulated under the School Law of 2006 in terms of general educational goals, core curriculum goals and measures of progression.

Status of the Implementation of the National Strategy

In 2009, the European Community Commission concluded in the *Digital Competitiveness Report*:

> "Denmark is among the top nations for most 2010 indicators, and is a clear frontrunner in the development of the information society. It is the leader in broadband penetration and has the highest share of frequent Internet users in Europe. With an action plan on green ICT launched in 2008, Denmark is also at the forefront in terms of eco-friendly usage of ICT." (European Commission 2009)

As early as 2000, Denmark had several frontrunner virtual- and blended mode master educations aimed at people in jobs. According to these educations' statistics, they proved to be successful in terms of learning quality measured as external, summative evaluations of students' performances, while alumni networks documented that the educations had a positive impact on the majority of students' careers. Additionally, a substantial body of research demonstrated that 'soft' competencies or ICT literacy, i.e. the ability to negotiate meaning and communicate in online environments, are essential teachers' competencies. This becomes particularly obvious in relation to the Humanities and Social Sciences, as these are characterized by weakly defined (Feltovich et al. 1996) and essentially contested concepts and problem areas (Connolly 1993). In contrast to these findings, and in contrast to general expectations, the research also documented that basic computer skills, i.e. the functional skills required to perform specific operations, and technology did not create serious barriers in every-day practice (Dirckinck-Holmfeld 2000; Laurillard 2002; Levinsen 2007a, Salmon 2002; Sorensen 2000).

Frontrunners (16%) Innovators & early adaptors (15%)	Integrate ICT in both the educational and the organisational setting.
Co-operating universities (33%) Early majority (34%)	Relatively far ahead in their ICT development process, especially in the organisational setting. Heavily involved in strategic co-operation with both domestic and foreign universities and with other education suppliers. Quite far advanced in integrating ICT in their campus-based teaching, while e-learning courses as such are offered only to a minor extent
Self-sufficient universities (36%) Late majority (34%)	Similar to the co-operating universities as regards ICT integration but have a larger group of sceptical teachers. Much less involved in co-operation with other universities or actors and place less emphasis on EU initiatives and new forms of co-operation. The Rambøll study found that these universities are engaged in strategic co-operation only to a very low extent. 28% of the self-sufficient universities are quite large, with more than 20,000 students each.
Sceptical universities (15%) Laggards (16%)	These universities are lagging behind the rest in almost all respects. They are characterised by limited use of all kinds of digital services. Additionally, only 13% of these universities have developed a formal ICT strategy. The attitudes towards ICT are mixed, with substantial numbers of teachers and management being sceptical.

Figure 2. Rambøll management report, university clusters.

Already before 2003, the universities' development contracts with the Danish government aimed at a broad implementation of the frontrunner experiences. However, a survey of the actual implementation of in-service competence development (Levinsen 2007c) showed that most offers were not adequate to raise the teachers' competencies above Dreyfus & Dreyfus' Advanced Beginner's Level (1986). In spite of the research findings, the main body of competence development courses was and still is basic computer-literacy courses. Subjects such as online pedagogy, ICT and designs for teaching and learning, online dialogue and CSCL composed and still compose an insignificant part of the competence-development programmes offered. These results are supported by the Rambøll Management Report for the European Commission (2004, pp. 10). The report divides European universities into four clusters (Figure 2) based on their integration of ICT: Front-runners (16%), Co-operating universities (33%), Self-sufficient universities (36%), and Skeptical universities (15%). The report concludes that the Danish universities are not frontrunners. The Rambøll-classification is based on Everett M. Rogers' Theory on Diffusion of Innovations (2005) and his categories: Innovators, early adaptors, early- and late majority and laggards.

These conclusions are reproduced in later empirical studies. Dørup et al. (2005) found that only a few Danish Master Programmes are in fact frontrunners according to the Rambøll/Rogers definition. Levinsen (2005a) found that the universities' strategies for implementing ICT were ill-defined, and that the in-service training for teachers displayed a low capacity pr. time unit. The courses prioritized basic introduction to technology and software while they neglected pedagogy and designs for teaching and learning related to online teaching, CSCL and general educational use of ICT. Levinsen (2005b) found that at the then 12 Danish universities, only 125 separate courses and 60 full educations (including Master Programmes) involved pedagogic use of LMS and e-learning. Few integrated CSCL in the pedagogic practice, while the majority of the courses and educations revolved around training procedural skills related to well-structured knowledge domains. Additionally, the majority of Danish university teachers were identified as belonging to Rogers' (2005) categories: *early majority, late majority*, and *laggard'* according to the adoption of ICT in their teaching practice. These teachers would use ICT and LMS because they had to and only to distribute course material and one-way information, and to receive students' submission of assignments.

The pattern from the universities was repeated in the Danish primary schools (Undervisningsministeriet 2005) where most of the teachers made little use of the possibilities of ICT and LMS (figure 3).

Despite the recent conclusions in the European Committee's Digital Competitiveness Report (2009) and the huge effort within substantial investments and government-supported development programmes, the pattern is still that the majority of teachers in the schools (EVA 2009) and at the universities do not use LMS or ICT as a pedagogical driver in the everyday teaching and learning processes and activities, and only a few Danish universities (or specific departments within universities) may be considered frontrunners according to Rambøll/Rogers definition.

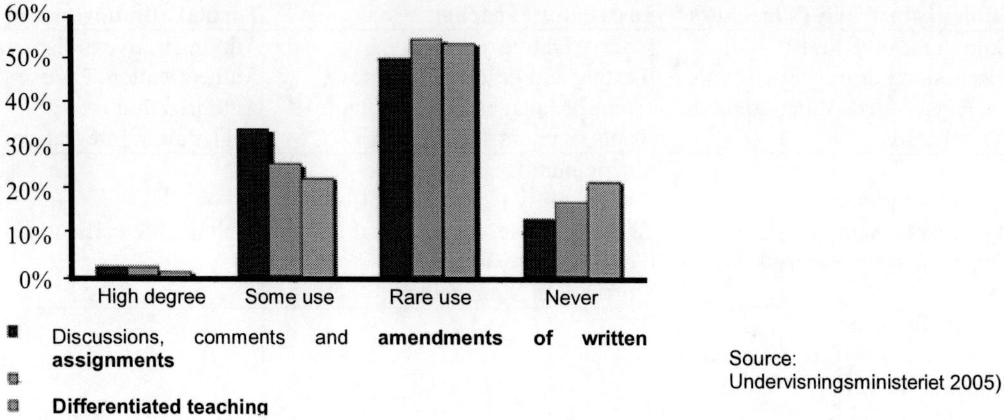

Figure 3. Pedagogical use of ICT in Danish schools (Representations produced by the author).

In order to improve the implementation of ICT, digital literacy and Web 2.0 in core curriculums, the universities' development contracts are being re-negotiated while the schools' general educational goals, core curriculum goals and measures of progression are at present being adjusted by an expert committee of which this author is a member (Hansen et al. 2009, Undervisningsministeriet 2009). The expert committee advised that the efforts are turned from technology and general implementation of ICT as the high priority towards two specific areas. First, the present strong focus on digital literacy (Martin 2006) has inspired the committee to suggest that digital literacy is implemented as four themes: 1) Information literacy and ICT; 2) Digital production and presentation competencies; 3) Analysis of digital communication and multimodal literacy; and 4) Communication, knowledge sharing and collaboration. These recommendations align with recent conclusions in Norway (Dannelsesutvalget 2009). Secondly, as the implementation of ICT have passed two phases: 1) Providing hardware and software; and 2) General implementation of ICT in designs for teaching and learning and focus on teachers' basic ICT literacy, the committee suggests a strong focus on pedagogic implementation of ICT in relation to core curriculum.

State of the Art - Features in Current LMS

In Denmark the universities are free to choose any LMS, while the schools are all (by governmental decision) part of a shared network based on FirstClass. A study of blended- and online university educations in Denmark (Levinsen 2007a) found that the different universities preferred different LMS, i.e. Blackboard, FirstClass, Sitescape, Virtual-U and LUVIT. The study also found a wide range of combinations of core curriculum, cross disciplinary topics, group sizes and designs for teaching and learning. Additionaly, the designs for teaching and learning varied from traditional instructivist teacher-centered practice to constructivist and social construtivist student-centered practice, while the actual use of LMS varied from simple document sharing to advanced blended learning and CSCL. The immediate conclusion is that the various LMS neither disadvantage nor promote specific pedagogies or designs for teaching and learning. Of course the users, both teachers and students, find certain LMS more user-friendly than others.

Students/instructors/teachers	Instructor /Teacher	Formal administration
Communicative tools: Discussion Forums, Email, File Exchange, Chat, Video, shared Whiteboard	Course Delivery Tools: Testing and grading, Helpdesk, Course Management, Grading Tools, Student Tracking	Administrative tools: Authentication, Course Authorization, Registration Integration
Productive tools: Bookmarks, Searching, Review, Help, Calendar, Progress	Curriculum Design: Accessibility Compliance, Content Sharing/Reuse, Instructional Design Tools, Course Templates, Curriculum Management,	Technical Specifications
Student Involvement Tools: Group work, Self-assessment, Student Community Building, Student Portfolios		

Figure 4. Commonly shared features by Learning Management Systems (Representations produced by the author).

There are only few studies of the adabtability of LMS in the literature. Graf & List (2005) used Qualitative Weight and Sum Approach and found that among 36 platforms, Moodle was the best suitable open source LMS from the perspective of adaptability regarding specific pedagogies, learning objectives, knowledge levels and learning styles of the individual learners. Brown, Paewai and Suddaby (2009) identified a series of pedagogical criteria in the literature and found that Moodle was the best choice for New Zealand's largest university-level distance education provider. The reason for these conclusions was that Moodle offers *learning-centredness*. That is, the ability to adapt Moodle to various pedagogical approaches where both acquisition and participation are allowed an important role in the educative process. These studies evaluate the LMS from the point of view of the students who participate and learn. However, neither evaluates the adaptability of the LMS to the teachers' ways of working or the teachers' need for tools to support students learning in various designs for teaching and learning. Levinsen (2003) analysed both commercial and open source products regarding adaptability from the teachers' point of view, using a comparative qualitative approach based on Edutools (http://www.edutools). Edutools is a non-commercial website that presents a large number of LMS in detail, including the ones used in Danish educational institutions except for LUVIT. Edutools allows the user of the site to compare all LMS in the database by features. The survey from 2003 was updated with samples from Edutool in 2009 where Moodle had also come into use at one Danish university. Figure 4 displays the condensed results of the comparative analysis of features in all LMS in the Edutool database and the table shows that most LMS share a majority of features.

Student/instructor/teacher-tools support communication, collaboration, coordination and group management, while *administrative tools* support organisational management of students and courses. The *instructor/teacher-tools* support customized and user-generated designs of teaching and learning environments and the actual carrying out of courses. Nothing in the features of the LMS restrict the choice of any pedagogy within the range from instructivist to advanced constructivist approaches. However, the design of the *survey*- and *evaluation-tools* is restricted to instructual pedagogy. It is found that most LMS offer a rich toolbox for constructing automated tests, e.g. variations over the form "teacher asks – student answers" and multiple-choice tests based on the basic assumption that any question has one and only one correct answer. The *student-tracking tools* produce reports on individual student behaviour in terms of information about the time and date for student activities; where the students have been in the system and for how long time, their repetition of material and exercises, together with failed or successful assignments within selected areas of the LMS (so called *instructual learning objects*). The LMS produce specified reports on students' efforts to fulfil assignments. Summaries of students' performances on assignments are also available. In conclusion, the nature of the reports points to the teachers' role as instructors, rather than the role as coaches and to a design for learning that is teacher centered rather than student centered. But, what is the problem for the ICT competent teacher who prefers a student centrered approach?

In constructivist and collaborative designs for teaching and learning, it is a precondition that learners work together in groups and that they explore the subject and negotiate meaning (Illeris 2006, Laurillard 2002, Salmon 2002, Wenger 2003). That is, they negotiate and define mutual areas of interest within the subject matter. They explore the problem area, identify problems and reflect on solutions, understanding and new knowledge. Most LMS support these activities through communication tools such as discussion boards, blogs, wikis and chat-fora. However the *survey-* and *evaluation tools* do not fit into constructivist designs for teaching and learning. In contrast to the traditional instructivist approach, there are no quantifiable or well-defined measures in collaborative learning that can be evaluated in multiple choice tests, because the reflective and explorative quality of the students' participation in the ongoing learning process is the focal point of the course evaluation (Sorensen & Takle 2002). Therefore it becomes relevant to ask how the features of current LMS influence the teachers' working conditions and the quality of the teaching.

Based on Russell Ackoff's Theory of Problem Solving (1974), instructivism and constructivist teachers' practice can be described through Ackoff's concepts: *reaction* and *proaction*. In instructional design for teaching and learning, the process follows a linear progression. If students do not fulfil the measures when tested, the reaction is to repeat the content and exercises, maybe in a slightly different way. In instructual design, this feedback loop is called *drill and practice* and instructors *react* on test results. As instructual design relies on measurable products rather than process, instructual teaching benefits from automation and digitalization may be regarded as a relatively straight-forward transformation. On the other side, constructivist teachers depend on personal and sensitive awareness of emerging tendencies during students' group work. They have to continuously construct and modify their basis for *proactive* decision-making on how to best coach their students. The actual place where teachers can observe empirical phenomena and detect emerging patterns and tendencies is where the students' activities leave marks in the LMS. Collaborative online courses organize students in various online activities, e.g. role-play and discussions (Salmon 2002, Sorensen 2002). In these setups the students reflect on and discuss the subject matter and the literature. In order to *proact* under these conditions, the teacher needs to observe the emerging tendencies and patterns that are embedded in the body of written or multimodal contributions. It could be gradual changes in the students' approach to learning in terms of surface vs. deep learning, communication patterns; patterns of collaboration, frequently used concepts, ways of posing questions etc. within and between groups (Levinsen 2007b). Awareness, negation of meaning and tendencies are processes that cannot be digitally automated. In order to be operational in the virtual environment, these processes rely on user-friendly semiotic user-interface representations and user driven interaction. Therefore, digitalization of constructivist and social constructivist designs for teaching and learning is far from straight-forward.

With a Danish average number of students in classes between 20 and 100, and course modules running for 2-4 weeks, the amount of asynchronous written or multimodal contributions is often vast, - 300-600 contributions corresponding to 60 to 160 normal pages (ibid.). Nobody can read this amount of contributions thoroughly, nor can the essences of the contributions be gasped through skimming. Multimodal contributions or synchronous written or video/voice communications do not ease the teachers' workload. Teachers may manage to follow and mediate discussions, but they can by no means detect emerging tendencies or patterns before they appear for all to see. Obviously, this may be too late if the changes evolve in unfortunate or undesirable directions. In current LMS, the emerging tendencies and patterns that are paramount for the constructivist pedagogic approach become invisible from the teachers' point of view. The reseach concludes that available *survey-* and *evaluation-tools* in current LMS including Moodle, do not support qualitative and formative evaluations of ongoing processes, nor do they support teachers' *proactive* decision-making. The lack of features that support teachers' formative awareness may affect the quality of the students' learning (Levinsen 2007a). These findings correspond to the few studies that look into the teaching and learning models of LMS and their influence on the teachers' acceptance of LMS (Apedoe 2005; Hedberg 2006; Naidu 2006). However, these studies draw the conclusion that teachers' reluctance towards the LMS is coursed by discomfort generated by the LMS' inherent pedagogy. These studies do not analyse and evaluate the adabtability, usability and interaction design of the LMS from a teacher's point of view.

In the following section, the actual consequences of interaction design and usability of current LMS are explored through a long-term case study from 2002. The author may have not been able to identify simular studies but where it has been possible, the case study has been updated.

LMS Asteachers Work Condition – A Case Study

The Case MIL

The case study followed the blended mode Danish Master in ICT and Learning (MIL) during the first semester in 2002. The new group of students counted 53 adults whose motivation was either to improve their job opportunities or current carrier through continuing education or to seek personal challenges. The research methods were primarily qualitative, and relied on anthropological methods such as observation at seminars, participation in online discussions and interviews. However, quantitative data concerning the relations between individuals, content, distribution, freqencies and numbers of contributions was also collected.

The semester, figure 3, began with an online introduction to the LMS and the students met twice at weekend seminars. At the first seminar, the large group was subdivided into 10 working groups. Each group was designated a private group space in the LMS. During the semester, the groups participated in two parallel modules, M1 and M2. M1 concerned learning theory and CSCL. The students were organised into various collaborative constellations by the teacher where they discussed the core curriculum in relation to roles and tasks. The students were evaluated on their qualitative and quantitative participation in the discussions (Sorensen 2003). The discussions took place in the M1 public conference.

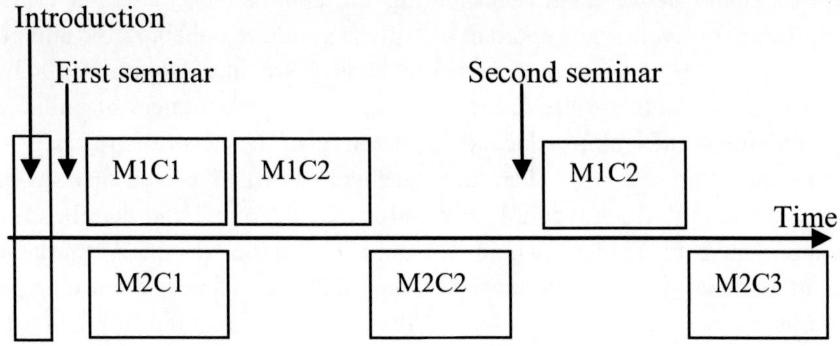

Figure 5. Semester schedule, MIL 2002. M refers to modules. C refers to courses within modules.

M2 concerned HCI (Human-Computer Interaction) and visual interaction design of interactive learning applications or environments. The teachers of M2 expected the students to organize knowledge-sharing in the public M2 conference while they worked on their assignments in the private group space. The teachers offered fixed periods of guidance. The students were evaluated summatively though written assignments at the end of each M2 sub-course. The final assignment was the design and user test of an e-learning application interface.

During the case study, the author was allowed access to all public conferences, and 5 out of 10 private group conferences. Further qualitative interviews established that 9 out of 10 groups used alternative virtual environments because they found the chosen LMS old-fashioned and inadequate to use. Therefore, the full extent of private group communication is unknown. In 2002, the chosen alternatives were Skype and MS Messenger. Today the alternatives include various collaborative and file-sharing Web 2.0 applications.

Analysis of Communication Among Groups in MIL

In 2002, MIL used Virtual U as LMS and since then Virtual U has been replaced by FirstClass. However, the change had no impact on the everyday online practice, because neither Virtual U nor FirstClass possess constructivist teacher support features. As the LMS did not offer any tools to filter contributions or to get an overview of all contributions, the author has manually produced a spreadsheet containing all participating students' individual contributions in all accessible discussion fora. This spreadsheet was used to analyze the body of contributions and allowed the author to simulate overview- and filtering tools for future LMS. The simulations revealed discrepancies between the teachers' impression of the quality of the ongoing discussions and the actual patterns of learning behaviour. Thus, the simulations demonstrate the consequenses of the fact that present LMS do not fully support the constructivist learning paradigm, and point at future improvements of LMS in terms of flexible and dynamic tools and views that support present awareness, meaning negotiation and proactive process management.

The whole semester produced 2244 contributions in the public conferences; 1917 contributions from M1 and 327 from M2. Questionnaires and interviews demonstrated that the students chose a cost-benefit strategy and placed their contributions where they expected the teachers to acknowledge them. Considering the summative evaluation criteria this is hardly surprising. However, it is important at MIL to promote collaborative and cooperative learning and knowledge-sharing as general methods (Dirckinck-Holmfeld 2002, Sorensen 2003), because the students are the future developers and practitioners of online education, software development and online educational planning in the networked society (Sørensen, Audon & Levinsen forthcoming). Therefore, teachers at MIL expected that students would always choose a strategy which would lead towards deep learning, and that the criteria of the mandatory summative evaluations would not impact their behaviour. A similar disturbing observation of students' cost-benefit strategies, one that often escapes the teacher's attention, appears when the freqency of contributions in discussions is analysed in relation to time. In this case, the teacher expressed satisfaction that all students participated in a written discussion running over two weeks. However, the analysis revealed that 25% of the contributions were submitted during the last two days of the course. Additionally, half of the group only joined the conference during the last 3 days, a fact that may explain why the majority of contributions never recieved any response. In the specific context, this analysis contradicts the teacher's impression that the students genuinly participated in a discussion. In general, the analysis raises the questions: What do we mean by genuine participation in discussions? and What do we mean by *quality of participation* as a parameter for summative evaluation?

Group number	1	2	3	4	5	6	7	8	9	10
Self Communication	27	13	17	9	12	46	42	79	11	60
All Contributions (1425)	133	116	115	106	80	181	186	188	59	261
Self Communication %	20 %	11%	15%	8%	15%	25%	23%	42%	19%	26%

Figure 6. The relation between the groups according to their self-communication.

An important element in the constructivist and social constructivist design for teaching and learning at MIL is that discussions and knowledge sharing take place both inside and between the working groups and it is generally assumed by the teachers that the students engage in distributed discussions. Therefore, another simulated filtering focussed on 'Who is talking to whom?' All contributions in public M1 and M2 conferences answering another contribution were counted. The initial contribution of each thread is not counted as they are not replies. When somebody replies to a contribution from their own group, it is called *Self Communication.* Figure 6 shows the frequency of Self Communication.

Even though all groups communicated with other groups, seven groups have got themselves as the preferred communication partner. The rest had themselves as number 4 or 5 most popular partner. The LMS, Virtual U and now FirstClass, does not provide any tools to bring forth this kind of data from the courses, and there are far too many contributions for the teachers to manage. However, this example demonstrates the need for proactive tools when teachers deal with collaborative and cooperative designs for learning, because these designs produce vast amounts of contributions, and they impact the construction of social relations within the large group over time.

Another point that may shed further light on the social construction at MIL and similar educations is the distribution of contributions from both public and group conferences. The distribution from the first semester 2002 shows that the students' communication was internal to their own groups, rather than knowledge-sharing in public between groups. Figure 7 shows high activity in the public M1 and the private M2 conferences. The private M1 conferences and the public M2 conferences both show low activity. The summative evaluation of M1 rests on participation in the public space while M2 is evaluated on a delivery at the end of the course. Therefore, the distribution in Figure 7 supports the above mentioned observation that students place their effort where the teachers acknowledge it. It also raises the question whether MIL's learning objectives are actually fulfilled. The collaborative communication patterns and knowledge-sharing, which MIL is designed to facilitate, succeeds in M1where it is demanded but is rare in other modules.

Group nr.	**1**	**6**	**7**	**8**	**9**
M1 public	159	265	262	255	82
M1 group	85	139	8	350	0
Sum total	**244**	**404**	**254**	**605**	**82**
M2 public	40	35	52	31	17
M2 group	161	455	263	982	236
Sum total	**201**	**490**	**315**	**1013**	**253**

Figure 7. The amount of contributions in public and group conferences in M1 and M2.

Does the pattern support the assumption that knowledge-sharing is actually limited at MIL? Does the pattern document that the different designs for learning at the two modules, M1 and M2, combined with the different forms of summative evaluation criteria actually influence the process of socialisation at MIL other than intended in MIL's overall design? This may actually be the case as the preference for limited knowledge-sharing continues as closed circuits of communication in the succeeding modules, and as students who choose to write the master thesis individually. The limitations in present LMS prevent the teachers from identifying any emerging trends or patterns in the first place. Recent samples at MIL show that the patterns are relatively unchanged and a recent study on the use of digital process-portfolios as mandatory criteria for summative evaluation supports the above assumptions. The students in this study use BlackBoard which can track numbers of visits to specific areas. The tracking reveals that the students look at fellow students' portfolios, but they do not comment on them (Orngreen, 2009).

A means to overcome the consequenses of the weak LMS' teacher tools were and still is to evaluate through quantitative measures of participation. In module 1 at MIL each student is asked to produce minimum 5 contributions and must in return receive response from other students on 2 out of at least 5 contributions (Sorensen & Takle, 2002). In 2002, the author's manual filtering of contributions and responses pr. person showed that more than 50% of the students balanced on the edge of the acceptable measures. The overall pattern for the semester showed that 20% of all students did not perform acceptably regarding this quantified summative evaluation criteria as more than 60% of their contributions were ignored. The simulated filtering allowed a closer look at ingored contributions which were found in two varieties: 1) A contribution may constitute the end of a discussion thread, or 2) a student may start a new tread that nobody reacts to. Without tools that can filter contributions according to their location in the discussion threads in relation to the sender, it is not possible to determine whether a student has a habit of posting conclusions rather than participate in the discussion, or whether a student is genuinely ignored. In this example the teacher cannot perform as coach and discuss with students back in the discussions. In other cases, rejection may be due to the ignored student's unfortunate approach to communication in the online environment. In this case, the teacher is excluded from helping the student to find more appropriate ways of communicating. The only way to produce the nescessary insight is that the teacher actually reads everything that is published in the discussions, which is out of the question due to the consequent heavy workload.

It is important to notice that the shortcommings of current LMS at MIL do not only impact the teachers' ability to proact in relation to unfortunate or undesireable emerging patterns and trends. The positive and excellent contributions may also be overlooked and drown in the 'information overload' that both teachers and students encouter in current LMS (Levinsen 2007a).

THE FUTURE LMS

The implementation of LMS in educational organisations in Denmark is based on high expectations and visions. The Danish government strives for world class performance and exploitation of ICT. However, the analysis of the current state of ICT-implementation from primary school to university level demonstrated that there is still a long way to go. Many teachers have not yet adapted ICT into their every day-practice. The use of LMS is limited to one-way information and distribution of documents. This chapter raised the question whether teachers' reluctance towards LMS is due to the poor usability and interaction design of the LMS, due to the level of the teachers' ICT related pedagogic competencies, or both. The study has demonstrated that some reluctance can be ascribed to the teachers. In Denmark there is a growing realisation that the current in-service training offers should change from traditional instructual courses (the so called *ICT drivers' license* courses') to more explorative and hands-on workshops, where self-directed learning (Knowles 1988), or what Martin (2006 p. 155) calls *a Repertoire of Digital Uses* and the *Ability of Digital Transformation,* is supported along with knowledge-sharing.

The analysis of features in current LMS showed that teachers who feel insecure are further alienated by the lack of adaptability, usability and user friendly affordance of the current LMS. As the case study showed, it is difficult to perform the pedagogy and designs for teaching and learning associated to the Networked Society. Even if the teacher is confident with ICT and is a competent performer of (social) constructivist designs for teaching and learning in virtual environments, current LMS do not facilitate the teacher in the role as a proactive coach, because any emerging trend or pattern, regardless of it being desirable or unfortunate, is invisible to the teacher. As it is, any teacher who wants to overcome the shortcomings of current LMS is challenged to choose between an enormous workload and a loss of quality. With the explosive development of Web 2.0 applications and services, the need for dynamic process management tools becomes even more urgent. Current attempts to meet the challenge within the research field Intelligent Tutoring Systems aim towards intelligent automation and expert systems. A substantial body of literature documents that similar solutions have proved inadequate in applications aimed at decision support in Business Management, while user-controlled interaction with dynamic filtering tools and interactive visual representations in Decision Support Systems and Data Mining Systems have proved more successful. Due to the similarities between teachers' and managers' needs when searching for information that may support sound decision making and proactive strategies, it is suggested that future development of LMS include research into the teachers' work conditions when they use LMS for constructivist and social constructivist designs for teaching and learning. It is necessary to identify and describe formative evaluation practices and the need for adaptable, dynamic, representative and interactive tools for proactive process management.

The author has, together with colleague Rikke Ørngreen from the Danish School of Education, coined the term *Proactive Teachers Tools* (Ørngreen & Levinsen 2004). Proactive Teachers Tools are not automatic or artificially intelligent. They are analytical tools analogue to tools known from the Data Mining and Decision Support Systems in Business Management. The idea is that these tools can provide various dynamic and interactive views on the emergence and development of relations with respect both to contributors and the production of content over time. Proactive Teachers Tools can help proactive teachers in their ongoing decision making about coaching strategies.

Talks to: \ Group nr.	**1**	**2**	**3**	**4**	**5**	**6**	**7**	**8**	**9**	**10**
1	27	14	12	12	6	9	17	9	4	17
2	10	13	17	16	1	20	14	11	1	26
3	12	9	17	8	14	9	19	7	5	15
4	8	7	11	9	3	28	4	7	2	12
5	6	6	6	4	12	14	7	4	3	12
6	11	19	13	26	11	46	14	14	5	35
7	12	10	13	8	13	16	42	21	11	37
8	11	11	10	6	0	12	16	79	10	21
9	24	4	2	3	2	4	14	12	11	17
10	12	23	14	14	18	23	39	24	7	69
Sum	133	116	115	106	80	181	186	188	59	261
Self comm.%	10	11	15	8	15	25	23	42	19	26

Figure 8. Who is talking to whom? (Dotted circles mark few and thick circles mark many contributions)

Network analyses such as 'Who is talking to whom?' may be visually represented as weighted relations of intensity, and changes in the relations should be visible over time. Figure 8 displays a weighted visual representation based on the simulated view from the MIL case study. The circles are hyperlinked to relevant master data and the written contributions in order to ease skimming and sampling of the material (Ørngreen & Levinsen 2005, fig. 1).

Another dynamic view combines the annotation method from hermeneutic analytical tools such as *ATLAS ti* with the students' use of keywords in their discussions. Figure 9 (Ibid figure 2) displays an example of such a view developed specifically for Case Based Learning (CBL). This view also supports the teachers' overview of the groups' prioritisations and how they annotate material in a case.

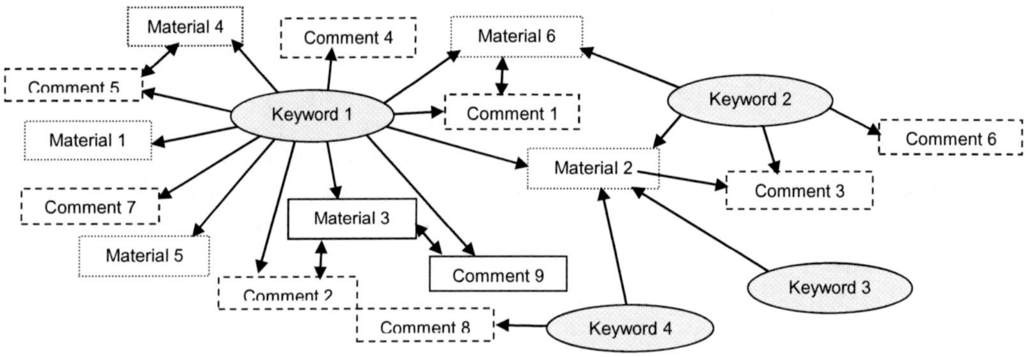

Figure 9. Suggestions for a dynamic view of annotations.

This specific view in Figure 9 has been developed for a prototype of the online application *CaseMaker* by Rikke Ørngreen and Copenhagen Business School Learning Lab.

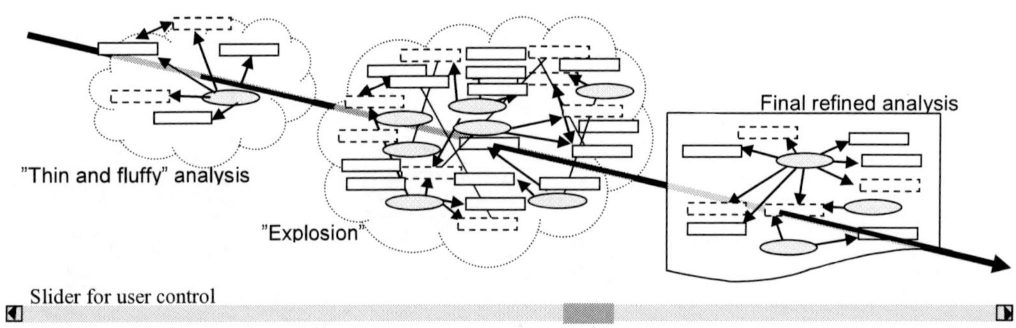

Figure 10. Suggestion for a dynamic animated view of annotation patterns over time.

Figure 10 (Ibid. figure 3) shows how a user-controlled time slider allows the proactive teacher to follow the progression of the students' analysis of a business case in *CaseMaker* from open exploration over the explosion of keywords and ideas to a structured and refined analysis.

Conclusion

The conceptual idea of the Proactive Teacher Tool is that all views are produced to support the proactive practice required in student centered constructivist and social constructivist pedagogy. The views are designed to allow the user to search the entire dynamic body of material in the LMS through user-controlled filtering tools and display the results in user-controlled representational forms. Each representational form contains visual markers of system generated, dynamic hyperlinks to the master data. The consequent dynamic web of information in the LMS may allow the proactive teacher to perform samples and to interfere in ways similar to face-to- face coaching. In this way Proactive Teacher Tools offer a virtual substitution for the lack of rich data that proactive teachers usually rely on in face-to-face situations.

Web 2.0 technologies develop rapidly, and it is now possible to use e.g. Word-clouds and MashUp technologies to produce this kind of user-controlled dynamic filtering in LMS and to support direct interaction and manipulation with the dynamic representations and selected data.

AUTHOR INFO

Karin Tweddell Levinsen is an associate professor in online education at university level at the Danish School of Education at Aarhus University. She is a member of the internationally acknowledged Research Programme on Digital Media and ICT in a Learning Perspective. Currently her research is focused on university pedagogy and ICT. Of special interest is the performative support that LMS/VLE may offer to dynamic CSCL based designs for learning and teaching practice. In a current project group KL works with the development of flexible LMS/VLE, where dashboard technology, web 2.0, open access and formal structures are combined into future resistant systems for educational institutions. KL has many years of experience as a professional user centred design developer of digital educational solutions, and she has been in the field since the two-screen solution and the laserdisc.

Associate Professor Karin Tweddell Levinsen, Ph D
The research programme of Media and ICT in a Learning Perspective
Department of Curriculum Research
Danish School of Education
Aarhus University
Tuborgvej 164, 2400 Copenhagen NV, Denmark
Tel: +45 8888 9491
Email: kale@dpu.dk
Web: www.dpu.dk/about/kale

ACKOWLEDGMENT

I thank the teachers and students at MIL 2002 for opening the door to their world to me and for being helpful in many ways. I thank my colleagues at the Danish School of Education – Aarhus University and especially Rikke Ørngreen for challenging discussions and collaboration.

REFERENCES

Ackoff, R. L. (1974). *Redesigning the Future*. New York, John Wiley & Sons.

Apedoe, X. (2005). The interplay of teaching conceptions and course management system design: Research implications and creative innovations for future designs. In A. Jafari & P McGee (Eds.), *Course management systems for learning: Beyond accidental pedagogy* (pp. 57-68). Hershey PA: Information Science.

Brown, M., Paewai, S. & Suddaby, G (2009). Moodle as a Trojan Mouse: Policy, Politics and Pragmatism, *Proceedings of the 8th European Conference on e-learning, Bari, Italy, 29-30 oct. 2009*, 100-107.

Connolly, W.W. (1993). *The Terms of Political Discourse*. Oxford: Blackwell.

Danmarks Statistik (2006). *Varige forbrugsgoder (Durables)*. Statistics Denmark.

Dannelsesutvalget (2009). *Kunnskap og dannelse foran et nytt århundre (Knowledge and general education in a new century)* ,[online report]), Dannelsesutvalget for høyere utdanning. Norway, *http://www.uib.no/filearchive/innstilling-dannelsesutvalget.pdf*

Dede, C. (2005). Planning for Neo-Millennial Learning Styles, *Educause Quarterly*, No.1, 7-12.

Dirckinck-Holmfeld, L. (2002). Designing Virtual Learning Environments based on Problem Orientated Project Pedagogy. In L. Dircinck-Holmfeld & B. Fibiger (eds.) *Learning in Virtual Environments* (pp. 31-54). Copenhagen, Samfundslitteratur.

Dreyfus, H. & Dreyfus, S. (1986). *Mind over Machine: The Power of Human Intuition and Expertise in the Era of the Computer*. New York: Free Press.

Dørup J., Gomme J., Hansen A. & Heiberg, B. (2005). Implementering af e-læring ved danske universiteter (Implementing e-learning at Danish Universities). In: *Tidskrift for universiteternes efter- og videreuddannelse*, 2 vol. No. 6, 1-13.

Edutools.com. *http://www.edutools.info/*

European Commission (2003). *eLearning: Better eLearning for Europe*, Directorate-General for Education and Culture, Luxembourg. Office for Official Publications of the European Communities.

European Commission (2004). *Key Competences for Lifelong Learning: a European Reference Framework*. Directorate-General for Education and Culture [online report] *http://europa.eu.int/comm/education/policies/2010/doc/basicframe.pdf*).

European Commission (2009). *Europe's Digital Competitiveness Report*, Volume 2: i2010 — ICT Country Profiles, Commission of the European Communities, Brussels

EVA (2005). *It på de gymnasiale uddannelser (ICT in the secondary school)*. EVA (Denmarks Evaluation Institute)

EVA (2009). *It I skolen –undersøgelse af erfaringer og perspektiver (ICT in the school - a study of experiences and perspectives)*. EVA (Danish Evaluation Institute).

Feltovich, P. J., Spiro, R. J., Coulson, R. L. & Feltovich, J. (1996). Collaboration Within and Among Minds: Mastering Complexity, Individually and in Groups. In Koschmann, T. (Ed.): *CSCL: Theory and practice of an emerging paradigm* (pp. 25-44). Mahwah, New Jersey. Lawrence Erlbaum Associates, Publishers,

G8 (2006). *G8 Wold Summit in St. Petersburg, July 16, 2006*. [online report], http://en.g8russia.ru/docs/12.html.

Graf, S. & List, B. (2005). An Evaluation of Open Source E-Learning Platforms Stressing Adaptation Issues. *Proceedings of the 5th IEEE International Conference on Advanced Learning Technologies (ICALT 2005),* 163-165.

Hansen, K. K., Hougaard, H. , Levinsen, K. T., Mikkelgaard-Jensen, L. & Sørensen, B. H. (forthcoming):.*4 temaer (Four themes).* Undervisningsministeriet (Ministery of Education).

Hedberg, J. G. (2006). E-learning futures? Speculations for a time yet to come. *Studies in Continuing Education*, 28(2), 171-183.

Heilesen. S. B. & Lerche Nielsen, J.(2005). Farvel til den "privatpraktiserende" lærer? (Goodbye to the closed-door teacher?). *Tidsskrift for Universiteternes efter- og videreuddannelse*, nr. 5., 1-15.

Illeris, K. (2006). *Læring (Learning)*. Frederiksberg, Roskilde Universitetsforlag.

Knowles, M. (1988). *Lifelong Learning: A Dream: Malcolm Knowles*. [online book], http://www.newhorizons.org/future/Creating_the_Future/crfut_knowles.html

Laurillard, D.(2002). *Rethinking University Teaching. A conversational framework for the effective use of learning technologies.* RuthledgeFalmer.

Levinsen, K. T. (2003). Klædt på som online-underviser – kommunikation som barriere for netstøttet undervisning (Ready for online teaching – communication as a barrier for CSCL), *LOM nr. 1 nov. 2003*, p 48-58.

Levinsen, K. T. (2007). Baby Boomers with Neo-millennial Learning Styles, *Proceedings of 2nd International Conference on e-Learning*, (ICEL 2007), Jun 28-29, 489-496.

Levinsen, K. T. (2007a). Qualifying online teachers - Communicative skills and their impact on e-learning quality. *Journal of Education and Information Technologies,* vol. 12(1), 41-51.

Levinsen, K. (2007b). Collaborative On-Line Teaching: The Inevitable Path to Deep Learning and Knowledge Sharing? *Electronic journal of e-learning*, 4 (nr. 1), 41-48.

Levinsen, K. (2007c). Watch out: the power users are coming. *Electronic journal of e-learning*, 5 (nr. 1), 79-86.

Marko, A. & Honkaranta, A. M. (2007). Bridging the Gap between Advanced Distributed Teaching and the Use of Learning Management Systems in the University Context. *Proceedings of icalt, Seventh IEEE International Conference on Advanced Learning Technologies (ICALT 2007),* 293-294.

Martin, A. (2006). A european framework for digital literacy, *Digital kompetanse*, nr. 2, 151-161.

Naidu, S. (2006). *E-Learning: A guidebook of principles, procedures and practices* (2nd ed.). New Delhi, Commonwealth Educational Media Center for Asia.

Oblinger, D. (2003). Boomers, Gen-Exers and Millennials: Understanding the New Students", *EDUCAUSE,* vol 38, 36–43.

OECD (2001). *Meeting of the OECD education ministers*, Paris, 3-4 April 2001 [online report], *http://www.oecd.org/dataoecd/40/8/1924078.pdf.*

Rambøll Management (2004). *Studies in the Context of the E-learning Initiative: Virtual Models of European Universities (Lot 1)*. Report to the EU Commission, DG Education & Culture

Reigeluth C. M. (ed.) (1999). *Instructional-Design Theories and Models*. Lawrence Erlbaum Associates,

Roberts, T. S. (2004).*Online Collaborative Learning: Theory and Practice*. Idea Group Publishing

Rogers, Everett M. (2005). *Diffusion of Innovations*, Glencoe: Free Press.

Salmon, G (2002). *E-tivities. The key to active online learning*. Kogan Page.

Sorensen, E. K. A (2003). Challenge in E. Orchestrating the Symphony of Collaborative E-Learning, *The International Journal of Innovations in Higher Education (IJIHE).*

Sorensen, E. K. & Takle. G. S. (2003). Learning through Discussion and Dialogue in Computer Supported Collaborative Networks. *Society for Information Technology and Teacher Education International Conference* Vol. 2003, Issue. 1. 2504-2510.

Steel, C. (2009). Reconciling university teacher beliefs to create learning designs for LMS environments, *Australasian Journal of Educational Technology,* 25(3), 399-420.

Sørensen, B. H., Audon, L. & Levinsen, K. T. (Forthcoming). *Skole 2.0 (School 2.0),* Aarhus, KLIM.

Undervisningsministeriet (2005). *Det Nationale Kompetenceregnskab,* Undervisningsministeriet (Ministry of Education) [online report], *http://pub.uvm.dk/2005/NKRresume/kompetenceregnskab.pdf*

Undervisningsministeriet (2007). *51.000 nye computere i folkeskolen (51.000 new computers in the primary school).* Copenhagen, Undervisningsministeriet (Ministry of Education).

Undervisningsministeriet (2009). *Fællesmål og trinmål (Official learning objectives and measures),* [Official online guide for primary and secondary schools]. Undervisningsministeriet (Ministry of Education). *http://www.uvm.dk/Uddannelse/Folkeskolen/Fag%20proever%20og%20evaluering/Faelles%20Maal%202009.aspx.*

Videnskabsministeriet (2007). *National strategi for IKT-støttet læring (National strategy for ICT supported learning),* Videnskabsministeriet (Ministry of Science, Technology and Innovation). [online report]. *http://www.itst.dk/filer/Publikationer/National_strategi_for_IKT-stoettet_laering/index.htm.*

Videnskabsministeriet (2009). English version of the Ministry of Science, Technology and Innovation's homepage, *http://en.vtu.dk.*

Wenger, E (2003). *Communities of Practice. Learning, Meaning and Identity*. Cambridge University.

Yale University (2003). *Yale University Report on Yale College Education,*[online report], *www.yale.edu/yce.*

Orngreen, R. (2009). ePortfolios in University and Blended Learning Settings, *Proceedings of the 8th European Conference on E-learning, Oct. 2009 in Bari, Italy,* 431-440.

Orngreen, R. & Levinsen, K. T. (2004). Proactive Teacher Tools – Enabling Teachers to Proact During e-learning Activities., *Proceedings of the 3 European Conference on e-learning, Paris Nov. 2004.* 569 – 579.

Orngreen, R. & Levinsen, K. (2005). Proactive Teacher Tools for Online Teachers. *Proceedings of The eighth IFIP World Conference on Computers in Education (WCCE2005)*, 4 – 7 July 2005, University of Stellenbosch, Cape Town South Africa 2005. 10 pages.

In: Interactive and Digital Media for Education in Virtual … ISBN: 978-1-61668-844-8
Editor: Cai Yiyu

Chapter 5

UNDERSTANDING THE REPRESENTATIONAL DIMENSION OF LEARNING: THE IMPLICATIONS OF INTERACTIVITY, IMMERSION AND FIDELITY ON THE DEVELOPMENT OF SERIOUS GAMES

S. de Freitas and I. Dunwell
Serious Game Institute, UK

ABSTRACT

Modern interactive digital mediums enable educational content to be represented in increasingly varied and sophisticated ways. An increasingly popular way of conveying this content is through 'serious games' – games created through a careful balance of modern entertainment game technology with instructional design concepts and pedagogies. The rapid emergence of this educational medium has proven particularly challenging for designers, who must achieve this balance in the face of few proven design approaches. de Freitas and Oliver (2006) advocate a 'four-dimensional' approach to this design challenge; coupled with a participatory approach which advocates involvement from learners in early stages of the development process, this model has provided a design framework for a number of serious games including *Triage Trainer* and *Patient Rescue*.

This chapter explores in more depth the 'representation' dimension of this framework. It is described as comprising three aspects, which together provide for immersive and interactive 3D virtual environments for training and learning applications. The main components of the representational dimension are discussed within this chapter as including interactivity with aspects of user control and selection, feedback and affect, immersion, with aspects of narrative and flow, and levels of fidelity, with higher fidelity levels often being associated with greater ease of learning transfer. Consequently, this chapter outlines a sub-theory of the four dimensional framework which seeks to frame a set of metrics that can be used to measure game and virtual world efficacy, and which may inform aspects of serious game mechanics and design.

Having defined in more detail the elements that constitute an effective representation of serious game content, this chapter applies it for validation into three diverse case study areas: Triage Trainer, the Rome Reborn project and Re-Mission. The three case studies set a context for discussion regarding the representation of serious games, and highlight some of the key issues and challenges associated with game-based learning and serious game design. Ultimately, this chapter raises questions serious game developers commonly face: to what level does content need to be represented to effectively realise pedagogies, and what gains can be achieved from investment in novel technology?

INTRODUCTION

As a convergence of technology and pedagogy, serious games represent a leading-edge medium for instructional content. The application areas for serious games are diverse; ranging from education and training through to health and the environment. However, a common theme throughout the sector is that serious games seek to address issues, which more conventional instruction techniques have struggled to address. Recurrent themes include reaching difficult target demographics, motivating and affecting learners, and conveying subjects conventionally seen as challenging or problematic areas for instruction. Serious games, therefore, represent the emerging hope that technology, combined with the expertise of game designers and instructors, will succeed in areas in which conventional methods struggle to deliver learning outcomes.

BACKGROUND

The four dimensional framework (4DF), originally described by de Freitas and Oliver (2005), suggests four key influencing factors that must be addressed in the development of a serious game. These elements are defined as the learner, context, representation and pedagogy. In the development of many games multiple dimensions are already fixed or constrained by the specification or available resources, for example, the demographic of learners targeted by the game are often specified prior to development and remain static throughout a project. Similarly, the context in which they learn – usually through keyboard and mouse interaction with a two-dimensional display, and with little direct intervention from instructors, is often inflexible. Thus, the dimensions which commonly offer serious game developers the greatest scope for innovation are the representation and pedagogy strands. Representation within the 4DF is defined in terms of how information is presented to the user, and thus considers the roles that different game engines, technologies, and interface designs can play, as well as the importance of aspects such as feedback medium and style. Pedagogy, by comparison, considers the underlying processes and paradigms by which learning is envisaged to occur during interaction within the game.

Both dimensions offer a range of complexities, not least in that they are interlinked and often changes or restrictions imposed on one dimension affect the other. This chapter intends to provide a step towards more fully understanding the representation dimension; a particularly relevant consideration as technology rapidly advances to offer an increasingly diverse range of technologies and interaction techniques for serious games, including handheld devices, augmented reality, mobile technology, and true three-dimensional imagery. Towards this end, the next section discusses the nature of the representation dimension, in terms of its constituent parts. These components are described under the broad headings of *interactivity*, *immersion*, and *fidelity*, chosen in part due to their prevalence amongst background literature. Collectively, these three considerations encompass the sophistication with which game content is realised, both visually and functionally, how users interact with this content, and also how they perceive it. Although conventional methods focus on three-dimensional worlds rendered on a two-dimensional display, using standard desktop interaction, this chapter discusses the implications of this approach, alongside potential avenues for capitalising on emerging technologies in order to represent virtual worlds in new and innovative ways.

THE REPRESENTATIONAL DIMENSION

The first step when considering representation within the 4DF is to define more precisely the scope and remit of each of the four elements of the framework. It should be noted representation is the purest technical element of the framework; whilst learners, contexts, and pedagogies are inherent considerations in the development of any educational material, it is in the way material is represented and conveyed to the user that has been most affected by the rise of serious games, and, more generally, the application of virtual worlds and web technologies.

We consider, then, representation to consist of the depth with which the learner can **interact** with the environment, the degree to which it is capable of **immersing** the learner, and finally the extent to which content can be represented in a realistic, high-**fidelity** fashion. Combined, these three criteria cover a broad range of serious games, as shown in Figure 1.

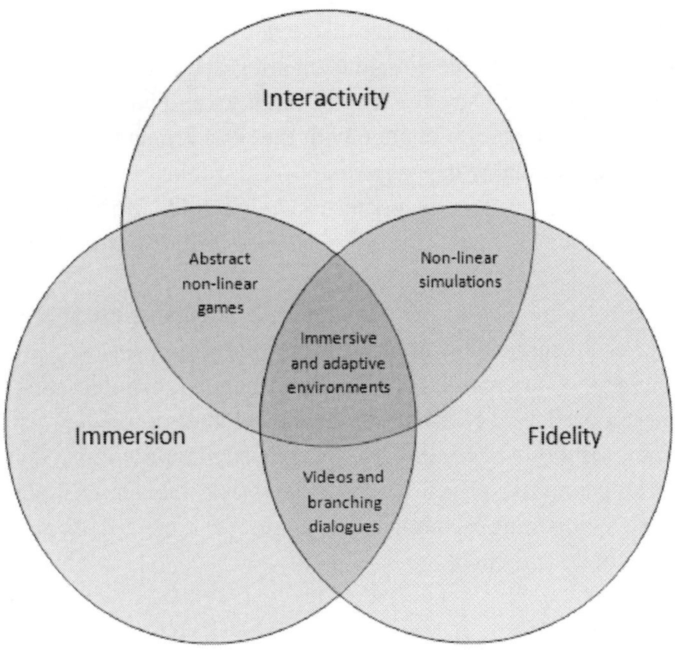

Figure 1. Immersion, Fidelity, Interactivity and Game Types.

The next sections discuss each of these three concepts in more detail. Specifically, we analyse how low-fidelity games may still immerse the learner through mechanisms such as narrative, and how interactivity encompasses not just the *action* of the player, but also the *reaction* of the world to their behaviour.

INTERACTIVITY

There is little question that interactivity lies at the core of any game experience. On a physical level, simple Newtonian physics models can add a depth of interactivity commonly seen in modern leisure games – objects fall, roll, bounce and react realistically to player actions. However, more recently, the capacity of games to replicate virtual ecosystems and microcosms using artificial intelligence techniques leads to the capacity to extend this action-reaction model to a deeper, social level. It becomes possible to convey feedback in terms of the impact on the world, rather than through a static screen. Through the use of such techniques, the learner is able to experience the consequence of their actions as they propagate through the game world, either realistically (e.g. *Ward Off Infection)* or in an abstract fashion (e.g. *Sneeze*). This approach supports the notion of 'sandbox' gaming, where the designer defines high level rules and game play emerges from the player interacting with the world in the context of this rule set, rather than as part of a highly linear experience.

This approach is often utilised to impact the affect of users: if a world is filled with plausible characters that the user identifies with, then the impact of their actions on these characters can evoke an affective response. Preliminary work with electroencephalographic technology and intelligent tutoring systems has supported this hypothesis (Rebolledo-Mendez et al., 2009), and the range of entertainment games that use narrative, consequential mechanisms to engineer affective responses also evidences the popularity of such approaches. For example, Valve's *Half-Life*, here in the opening sequence of the game, the player is placed into a 'late for work' scenario that can be readily - and generically - identified with. As a result, the player is encouraged to engage with the world in an everyday fashion, and when a 'disaster' occurs in the virtual world, as a direct result of the player's actions, the experience has primed the player to feel it is occurring in *their* world. More recently, games such as Bethesda's *Fallout 3* have implemented scenarios with multiple, morally ambiguous solutions.

Converting these techniques to serious games, particularly given the prominent role of affect in learning, is an interesting area for future development. A central issue faced by instructional designers when creating sandbox environments is integrating effective learning into the experience, a particular challenge since the greater the freedom users have to explore and develop unique solutions to challenges, the greater the possibility that they will deviate from planned learning activities. Even with this drawback, the demonstrated potential of such approaches to create compelling leisure games suggests that their application in serious games is a key area for future development.

Feedback

The challenge in enacting effective feedback mechanisms within serious games is in considering it from the perspective of both the game and instructional designer, pedagogically-oriented feedback mechanisms are only likely to be useful if they operate synergistically with game play elements. Similarly, game feedback should be carefully aligned to learning objectives; failure to do so results in the learner developing strategies to 'beat the game' without achieving the specified learning objectives (Binsubaih, 2008). Feedback has been shown to be a highly influential element of a successful serious game (Jarvis and de Freitas, 2009). In the evaluation of the *Triage Trainer* serious game, subjects reported that detailed feedback on performance left them unsure of their weaknesses and a simplified and more frequent feedback system yielded improved learning transfer.

If games are used as part of an instructor-led programme, then the instructor may be tasked with providing effective feedback. However, a key advantage of game-based learning is large-scale deployment without the need for human instructors, and, therefore, the ability of games to feedback effectively in an autonomous fashion is desirable. Although the role of automated feedback in serious games has been repeatedly shown as critical to delivering learning outcomes in the absence of an instructor, comparatively few studies have used empirical approaches to suggest the most appropriate techniques for a given scenario. The fact feedback in a prominent component of both gaming and learning underlines its dual role in serious games – as a central part of both the gaming and learning experience.

Rogers (1951) defines feedback as falling into five categories with increasing efficacy, a model which has been broadly adopted and analysed during the last half-century. Within the model, he identifies the three most commonly used methods as *evaluative*, *interpretive*, and *supportive*, with further, higher levels of *probing* and *understanding*. These methods of feedback can be seen in various incarnations in serious games; for example:

- Evaluative: You got a score of 120/200
- Interpretive: You got a score of 120/200 because you failed to respond quickly enough
- Supportive: You got a score of 120/200, and need to improve your response times to challenges
- Probing: You got a score of 120/200, because your response times were too low, was this because the user interface was too complex, or due to the game being too hard, or was it something else?
- Understanding: You got a score of 120/200, because you found the user interface too complex, and as a result you responded too slowly to the challenges, you should complete the tutorial on the user interface.

Enacting each level autonomously infers an increasingly ambitious level of technical development, influenced also by the complexity of the activity itself. For example, a game in which the user has to rapidly press a button in response to an on screen warning is simpler to analyse in terms of the causes of failure than a non-linear simulation, in which many potential actions may lead to similar results. Except in the simplest cases, Rogers' higher levels of probing and understanding feedback are primarily in the domain of artificial and evolutionary intelligence or human intervention; realising these methods fully requires either a human element to training simulations or artificial intelligence beyond the state-of-the-art.

Immersion

Csikszentmihalyi's (1991) concept of *flow* has been long-considered a central component of effective individual learning experiences. In a flow situation, a user is considered to be completely focused on the task at hand, and resistant to distractions. It is, then, easy to see the appeal of inducing such a situation within game-based learning, and equally simple to see the analogies to entertainment gaming, which can often focus the user on a task and achieve such an experience. For a serious game, the difficulty is often in ensuring the direction of this flow is towards a learning objective, rather than towards an abstract, and often irrelevant, mastery of the game.

Multiple independent studies (Roussos et al., 1999; Tashiro and Dunlap, 2007) reinforce an appreciation of *narrative* by providing engagement and structure within the learning process. Conventional narratives are linear; a traditional novel has a start point, end point and no deviation between the two. Although exceptions in literature occur – an example being the *Fighting Fantasy* (Jackson and Livingstone, 1982) series of books – written media is inevitably and unavoidably constrained to some level of linearity due to its nature. Authors traditionally develop their storytelling skills within this linear model, and as a result often adopt linear techniques when enacting game narratives. Many serious games adopt branching dialogue or narrative models, where choices from the user lead to different paths through a static narrative. These enable a degree of freedom, but since the options in these approaches are defined by the creator rather than the learner, they impede creative thought and problem solving as well as limit the ability of the user to explore the world.

Gaming, by comparison, has seen a steady progression towards experiences where the core, linear narrative is secondary or inconsequential to the game play itself. Successful examples include Rockstar Games' *Grand Theft Auto* series, which allow the player to simply ignore the narrative and objectives given by the game, and explore and interact with a virtual city as they wish. Similarly, even more conventional first-person shooters, such as Crytek's *Crysis*, have thrived on the implementation of scenarios and situations in which success can be achieved through many approaches, and the role of the game designer is in the implementation of the high-level rules and artificial intelligences that can adapt to the wide range of potential actions by the player.

Reflecting on the values of both approaches is essential when considering the design of a serious game experience. Linear narratives, which have been at the very core of human culture and social interaction for thousands of years, are challenged by emergent digital media that allow situations which would previously only have been imaginable to be given shape, form, and substance. It is this ability for electronic games and simulations to take storytelling a step further – to enter into and interact with the *imagination* of the user – that entails a new, relatively unexplored approach to describing situations and scenarios.

This brings with it a host of questions. Will a user, or indeed group of users, in the absence of a direct narrative, be eager to create their own narratives, and, if so, will these meet the expectations of the designer? This is even more relevant in serious game situations where these expectations underpin and reflect the learning requirements, which, if unmet, render the game ineffective. Even if the environment is conducive enough to enable the learner to construct and experience their own story, whether this will be as effective and appealing as a tightly-structured, professionally-written narrative remains a question. Real-world theatre productions such as Coney's *A Small Town Anywhere* has shown a willingness, and, indeed, enthusiasm for audience participation in a way which could easily be realised within a shared virtual space, but designing these experiences in such a way that learning requirements are effectively met represents a unique and complex pedagogic challenge.

Another question is how closely the objectives and elements at the core of successful games truly align to those of education. Many games use a host of mechanisms to promote long-term involvement from players, such as leaderboards, social networks, and, as mentioned, non-linear narratives that increase replayability. However, from an educational standpoint, rapid and efficient transfer of learning outcomes is often key. From this perspective, the *less* time a learner needs to play and interact with a serious game to achieve learning outcomes, the better. More open, exploratory, and non-linear scenarios imply greater completion times, both because there is increased potential for the learner to deviate from the 'correct' course of action, and less immediate feedback to the user that their actions are incorrect. Therefore, even though non-linear approaches are a major focus of the entertainment gaming industry, the benefits they bring to serious gaming should be carefully evaluated from an educational perspective.

A potential solution is to involve an instructor or educator within the virtual space to manage and direct learners in a way analogous to a real-world training or teaching environment. Whilst a skilled educator can address or ameliorate many issues associated with the deviation of learners away from learning requirements in exploratory environments, this is a solution which fails to exploit the potential for large-scale deployment of an electronic game. A much more demanding but powerful solution is one in which artificial intelligence is used to interact with, and learn from, the user, and autonomously ensure an effective learning experience.

Fidelity

Fidelity has been explored in a number of existing contexts – for example the visual nature of the environment can have a demonstrable effect on the affect of learners (Knez and Neidenthal, 2008), and this in turn has an effect on the learning process as a whole (e.g. Kort et al., 2001). Tashiro and Dunlap (2007) consider the impact of visual realism on learning engagement in educational games; in doing so they propose an isolation of learning, engagement, and realism as three mutually dependant variables. Their results reinforce the more general notions presented by Bogost (2007): that realism arises from narrative as well as visual fidelity, and that it is possible to wholly abstract a game design from its visual representation and narrative context.

Fidelity within virtual environments represents a key consideration of the representation dimension of the 4DF. In the specific case of simulators, for decades the goal has been to create high-fidelity environments on the assumption that the higher the fidelity of a simulator, the greater the efficacy of learning within it. Much evidence suggests process-based knowledge transfer benefits from more realistic environments in which to practise it (Park and Allen, 2005; Davidovitch, 2009), however, as real-time photorealism becomes increasingly achievable, the scope for considering if this 'more is better' approach holds universally true is increasing. Longhurst et al. (2006) themselves plainly demonstrate the limitations of human senses and perception; in an example users are asked to attend to a cup of pencils and perform a simple counting activity during a pre-rendered fly-through of a virtual scene, then asked what colour the carpet was. High failure rates to give the correct answer allude to the underlying, far broader issue of perceptual limitations affecting how rendered content as perceived, understood, and learnt from – visibility does not imply perception, as phenomena such as change blindness clearly demonstrate.

Much as advanced rendering approaches such as those of Yang and Chalmers (2005) have sought to consider perception, and, more specifically, perceptual limitations, advanced learning environments must not only take these limitations onboard, but they must also reflect upon the nature of the learner and how the salience of world content and elements contribute towards the learning experience - for example, how information placement can be used to cue the learner through an environment and mask its limitations

It can easily be concluded that the level of fidelity must match the desired learning outcomes. However, performing this matching is a complex task which requires the designer to reflect upon the nature of the learning requirements, and which elements of the environment contribute towards, or distract from, these requirements.

CASE STUDIES AND ANALYSES

The first of these case studies is Triage Trainer, a game developed by a leading entertainment games company, with expert input from medical practitioners and instructional designers. The game seeks to educate first-responders in the aftermath of an emergency in a city centre, particularly targeting scenarios in which real life training is both costly and difficult to apply effectively. The second case study, the Rome Reborn project, is an ongoing research initiative at the Serious Games Institute (SGI). The project intends to integrate a combination of leading-edge game technologies to provide a highly immersive, adaptive, and responsive learning environment. The future role that this combination of technologies could play in advancing the breadth and depth of the representation dimension is considered in this section, and we discuss some early emergent themes in relation to the representational dimension. The third case study follows, Re-Mission, a game targeted at young people with cancer and developed by the US charity HopeLab, which considers the representational dimension in relation to their evaluation.

Triage Trainer

Developed as part of the Technology Strategy Board-funded Engaging Training Simulations project, *Triage Trainer* was created by TruSim (a Division of Blitz Games), with input from Selex Systems Integration and Coventry University.

Triage processes are often taught using a 'Triage Sieve' approach, which centres upon correct 'tagging' of casualties at the scene into priority groups based on their condition. The training challenge emerges when attempting to create environments which allow learners to practice and rehearse the process in a realistic environment, low-fidelity approaches, such as table-top card games are commonly used, as are real world recreations using actors. Both these approaches have challenges either from difficulty in recreating the pressure and environment in which the skills are practiced, or presenting high costs and an inability to create scenarios which can easily be recreated or structured around the learner (e.g. Chen et al., 2008).

Fidelity

Triage Trainer sought to address training challenges through the implementation of a three-dimensional scene which recreates the aftermath of a bomb explosion in a major city. The learner was originally tasked with navigating through the scene to each patient, then performing the triage process as described by the triage sieve approach. Following the process, the learner was then presented with feedback on the accuracy and speed with which they performed the process. Several key lessons were learned from early prototypes (Jarvis and de Freitas, 2009):

- That the target users, being broadly unfamiliar with leisure games, struggled to navigate through the environment and became easily frustrated with the navigation approach (one common to leisure games). As a result, the game was modified to an 'on rails' approach, whereby the viewpoint moves automatically. This was better received by learners, aligning more closely to the learning requirement of triage process and speed than environmental navigation.
- That feedback was centrally important, both in terms of its nature and frequency. A second iteration of the game which increased the simplicity and frequency of feedback was well-received by focus groups.

These findings highlighted a number of relevant points to consider with respect to the fidelity of game content. Firstly, although adding more detail to the game world can have immediate visual impact and engage learners, if this is done without regard to the learners, and learning requirements, it can result in an overwhelming and disorienting environment. As visual realism increases, so do expectations of functional realism, and unless carefully managed these can leave users confused as to how they can interact with the world.

Immersion

In *Triage Trainer*, visual fidelity was intended as the primary tool with which to immerse learners. It demonstrates how the use of leading entertainment game technologies and assets can be used to create effective learning environments that utilise leisure game concepts to immerse the player, such as the integration of sound, colour and emotive content. With respect to the latter, there is little question that the real-time deterioration of wounded virtual patients provides a powerful and compelling example of the potential for games to recreate scenarios in ways that may even surpass real-world actor-based recreations.

Perhaps one of the most significant findings from the development of *Triage Trainer* was the need for more empirical studies into the efficacy of games and, in particular, individual key game elements such as feedback, to gain a better understanding of their role and impact on the learning process. Preliminary work has suggested individual game elements, such as score-based feedback, Leader boards, and win-lose ('game over') scenarios have dramatic, but often widely varying, impacts on game design and learning outcomes. Gaining a better understanding of how these elements work with both game play and instructional levels across a broad range of representation mediums is a vital area for future work.

Figure 2. Triage Trainer creates a triage situation within an urban setting.

Interactivity

Again, the modification to an 'on rails' movement system emphasizes the impact other dimensions of the 4DF can have on the way virtual worlds are represented as learning environments. Interactivity is closely coupled to ease-of-use, and high levels of interactive potential can also place mandates on the level of user expertise required to interact satisfactorily with the world. Although modern virtual environments can have high visual and functional fidelities, interaction, stymied by the common keyboard-mouse or game controller interface may still struggle to generate a true 'hands-on' experience.

Evaluation of the game as a whole, with 97 learners split into two groups within a pragmatic controlled trial gave promising early indicators of the efficacy of the game-based approach. Chi^2 analysis showed tagging accuracy was significantly higher within the game group ($p=0.02$). Step accuracy (the order in which checks were performed) was also higher in the video game group but only for the numbers of participants that followed correct procedure when triaging all 8 casualties (p=0.007).

Roma Nova

The *Roma Nova* project, undertaken by the Serious Games Institute's applied research group, seeks to explore both the pedagogy and technology that will underpin next-generation learning environments. To facilitate this exploration, the project brings together a number of key assets:

The *Rome Reborn* model, (Guidi et al., 2005) represents the most high-fidelity digital model of an ancient city currently in existence. The model includes large-scale terrain, walls and residential area components, as well as detailed internal and external models of the most prominent structures such as the Colosseum, Forum, Ludus Magna and Basilica of Maxentius.

- Spoken dialogue, facilitated through the ATOM engine, and combined with the expertise of researchers at the SGI in artificial life and evolutionary intelligence to create an intelligent tutoring system which can communicate to the learner naturally and intuitively.
- Crowd support through a 'Levels of Interaction' technique, which draws on analogous processes for levels of geometric and simulation fidelity providing not only complex interactions with nearby characters, but also a 'living background' that seeks to immerse the user in an environment populated by hundreds of other individuals. The behaviour of these characters will be driven by artificial life processes which allow characters to adapt and respond to many different user interactions, ranging from navigating through a crowd to stopping and interrogating individuals on their activity and knowledge.
- Pedagogies which support truly non-linear learning experiences, and encourage the learner to explore the environment in a situated context. Themes that will be researched include the analysis and definition of the key contributory factors towards immersion in an educational context, the value added by various game elements, and the nature and role of feedback in non-linear learning processes.

To address these objectives requires depth of both technical expertise and pedagogic understanding.

Fidelity

The *Roma Nova* project will explore the boundaries of visual and functional fidelity, and their interrelationship, in a range of novel ways. On a technical level, integrating a large-scale model within a game engine is a demanding task, requiring both labour-intensive refinement and processing of geometry, as well as the implementation of Level of Detail approaches in such a way as to provide visually satisfactory results. Preliminary work has seen elements of the model, including the Forum, successfully visualised within the Quest3D engine. Use of this engine has enabled the rapid implementation of a range of sophisticated lighting and environmental effects, including weather effects, shadows and physics. This engine will ultimately be used to create a full-scale, authentic recreation of Ancient Rome, which can be explored by the learner. Foremost in this recreation is the procedural generation of thousands of artificial, evolutionary-intelligence driven characters which can all be fully interacted with and exhibit crowd behaviours. This will be achieved through the aforementioned Levels of Interaction technique, applying spoken dialogue as well as evolutionary behaviour to create an adaptive and interactive crowd on both small and large scales.

Immersion

As well as leveraging the advantages of high degrees of fidelity to provide immersion, the project reflects upon the relationship between fidelity and learning requirements, and the analysis of specific game and pedagogic elements with respect to their impact on learners. In particular, the extent to which game-based elements such as scoring, missions, and success/fail conditions, supported by feedback, can influence and enhance learning outcomes is of interest. The mechanism through which these improved outcomes are achieved, be it greater immersion, motivation, engagement, or a combination, is also a topic of study.

Interactivity

One way in which the *Roma Nova* project is seeking to push the boundaries of interaction is through the seamless background integration of web-services to provide information to users in-world in novel ways. By reflecting the virtual world in terms of real world coordinate systems, multiple information systems, including GoogleEarth and GeoWiki can be queried and the information used to autonomously generate a wide range of data on locations based on available web sources. This can then be filtered back to the user in immersive and intuitive ways – for example through the spoken dialogue of a virtual character.

Such approaches, which forego the overheads and limited expansibility of learning environments created by subject matter experts in favour of links to the wealth of web-based content, promise to create learning environments which are less restricted and more dynamic in the way they source information and convey it to learners. In this context, the role of subject matter experts and designers is devising ways to best filter and present information, rather than generating it. This has significant potential for implementation in future learning environments, allowing them to scale autonomously as available information sources on the web increase, and removing the need for intervention by experts to update and extend the dynamic environment.

As a whole, the project will explore the potential of high-fidelity content to convey interactive experiences which immerse learners in a content-rich environment. Defining and understanding the most effective mechanisms by which learning can occur in these environments is a focal point of the research, contributing towards research which can inform designers at the earliest possible stage which game and instructional elements are best suited to a given set of learning requirements.

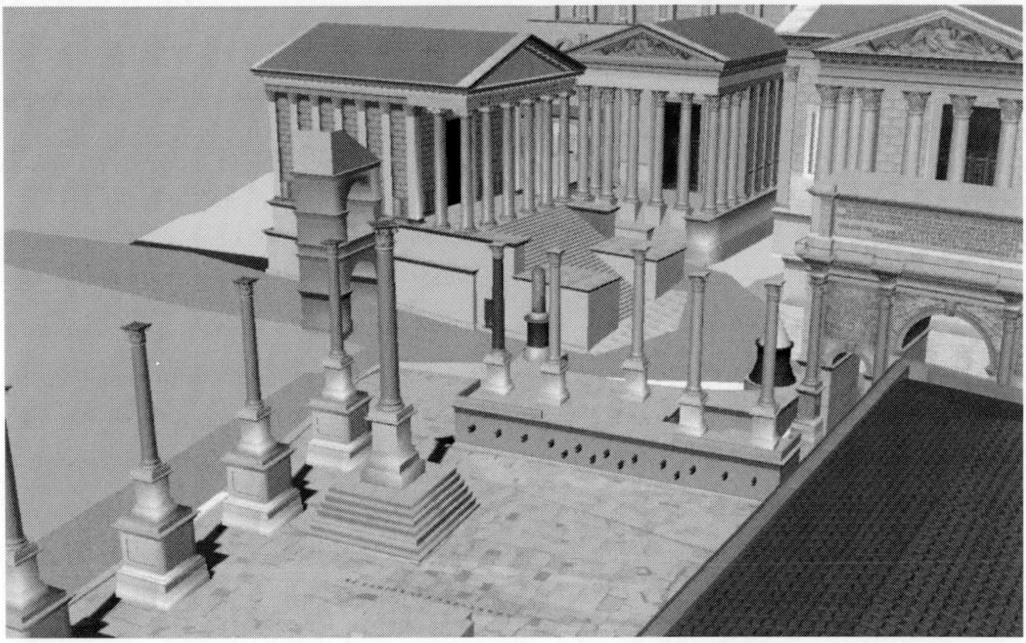

Figure 3. Roma Nova realises the Rome Reborn model within a modern game engine (Quest3D).

Figure 4. Real-time interactive rendering of the entire model using Java, showing the Tiber river (bottom right) and Colosseum (top right) as well as many other prominent structures.

Re-Mission

Re-Mission is a game developed by HopeLab (www.re-mission.net) for young people with cancer to encourage them to take their medication. The outcome of a recent randomised controlled trial (RCT) has shown positive results regarding medication adherence even in patients that only played the game for 1 hour. The study compared the Re-Mission game against a control video game and involved 375 cancer patients aged 13-29 years old at 34 clinical sites in Australia Canada and the United States. The success of the game in terms of behavioural change and the rigorous evaluation of the game have led to its selection for this book chapter.

Fidelity

According to the papers (Kato et al., 2008; Tate et al., 2009) published about the game, Re-Mission achieves behavioural change. Research at HopeLab has centred upon 'specific psychological pathways by which Re-Mission impacts health-related behaviour in adolescents' (Tate et al., 2009). While 'behavior-change components were originally engineered using a cognitive-behavioral approach' their recent observations indicated that non-cognitive processes also play a role. This has obvious implications upon the level of fidelity needed within the game to support behavioural change in the game players. The study found that 'changes in self-efficacy were more strongly associated with changes in behaviour than were changes in knowledge'. This has been supported by other studies outlined above (e.g. Jarvis and de Freitas, 2009).

Probably most notably from the study, despite the game's 20 levels:

> ...there was no relationship between the duration of game play (i.e. information exposure) and the magnitude of behavioural change (e.g., medication adherence), implying that short amounts of game play can induce rapid qualitative change in players' conceptions of themselves or their disease, ultimately leading to behaviour change (Tate et al., 2009, p. 30).

The level to which fidelity provided a part of the process of behavioural change was not tested in this evaluation, however the levels of fidelity to true life are evidently not part of the game design, which is clearly based upon a "shoot em' up" style game, where the illness and the power to overcome this are metaphorical rather than literal. The power of the game play here therefore rests less upon the fidelity to real world processes and more upon the power of games as a metaphor for supporting behavioural changes.

Immersion

The levels of immersion in the game are considered and the game as a whole adopts 20 levels. One of the significant challenges for the game developers was to reconcile the needs of the game appeal from the games development side and the need for biological accuracy and scientific evidence from the health professionals' side. To maintain the right balance the team defined core game design values (Tate et al., 2009):

- Choose a target health outcome
- Identify its key behavioural mediators
- Define the psychological determinants of behaviour
- Capture that perceptual field in the game-play scenario...
- Live out the contingencies in the virtual world instead of real life
- Always have fun (Behaviour=Knowledge x Motivation)

The team found that fun is an important aspect of motivation; the more fun the learner has the more they will play the game. The balance between game design and instructional and subject matter expertise is an important balance to get right with serious game design. While successful games such as America's Army have demonstrated this, designers such as Zyda (2005) have stressed the importance of maintaining strong game play whilst introducing instructional elements rather than attempting to integrate game elements within existing instructional designs. Immersion is an essential aspect of maintaining the motivation of the learners and hence measuring the success of the game play in achieving the learning outcomes, and an integral aspect of immersion is the levels of interactivity of the game.

Interactivity

The interactivity of the game in Re-Mission is substantial; the metaphor of the game and fighting cancer is a major aspect of the game design and mechanics adopted. At Level 1 Roxxi is attacked by an enemy lymphoma cell in the lymph node of the patient, and a colony of cells lurk in the background (see Figure 5). The player has to combat the enemy cells. Several of the game levels illustrate patients' in-game fighting leukaemia. Because non-adherence to prescribed medications is a behavioural mediator of mortality in adolescent leukaemia patients, several game levels were designed to involve missions in which Roxxi must discover and battle residual leukaemia cells still lurking inside the body (Tate et al., 2009: 31).The game adjusts in this way to the player and in instances where the in-game patient has skipped a chemotherapy dose Roxxi's chemo-concentrating blaster fires inconsistently allowing cancer cells to escape and to become drug resistant.

The interactivity of the game aids to empower the player through giving control over Roxxi and undertaking missions, reinforcing the need for adherence to medication, and thereby changing behaviour and supporting the efficacy of the patient. Together the fidelity (in this case trueness to patient medication patterns), the immersion (how absorbed the player becomes) and the interactivity (how much control the player has over the game play scenarios) together reinforce behavioural changes and lead to compliance of medication usage.

Overall the game evaluation was extremely positive confirming that games can be behaviourally changing and although challenging to design operate to support and develop motivation in learners and provide significant amounts of player empowerment.

Figure 5. Re-Mission uses an action game format to educate and entertain adolescents with cancer.

Discussion

Throughout this chapter, we have discussed the factors that impact upon how worlds are perceived, learnt from, and interacted with by users. From a design standpoint, the ability to utilize this discussion, alongside the handful of empirical studies that exist, is useful in creating informed serious game designs. Therefore, in this section, we attempt to collate this discussion and existing research to a model which may offer some avenues for consideration when creating and adapting serious games to meet learning requirements. Many of the issues touched on in this chapter – such as the role of immersion and components of an immersive experience, the relevance of fidelity and its relationship to both perception and learning requirements, and the potential of games to create immersive environments in which flow situations arise naturally, demonstrate a clear need for more empirical studies such as those of Kato et al., (2008), showing their efficacy and role within the learning process in measurable terms.

These case studies have presented several current and next-generation serious games and game platforms. The role of modern game engines in providing core technologies, APIs, and code bases upon which to efficiently build serious games is an emergent theme. *Triage Trainer* benefited extensively from Blitz Games' expertise as leisure software developers, and there are clear parallels between the need to simulate injuries and disasters for educational purposes, and leisure game content. Similarly, the *Roma Nova* project is bringing together a host of state-of-the-art assets within a modern game engine to create a next-generation serious game experience. Of particular interest within this project is the use of assets originally created for other purposes; the *Rome Reborn* model was originally. The development of Re-Mission also highlighted the need for the game to be comparable to current leisure game equivalents in order to appeal to its target audience.

CONCLUSIONS

In this chapter, we have presented a number of representational considerations for serious games, and discussed the importance of the role representation plays when developing and defining pedagogies which fully exploit and realise the potential and limitations of new technology. A particular point which has been discussed is that, although advances in game technology allow increasingly sophisticated environments to be created, pushing the boundaries of interaction, immersion, and fidelity, the extent to which any of these three representational components is realised must be driven by an underlying pedagogy and set of instructional design principles. Failure to do so risks creating experiences in which the user may suffer from 'information overload' (Warburton 2008); or deviate from the learning process.

That said, and considering viewpoints such as Zyda's - that game play must come before pedagogy - any serious game developer whose goals lie in reaching demographics unresponsive to other methods must be savvy of the representational advances in entertainment gaming. Effective games reaching this demographic must compete with leisure games for screen-time, and since budgets typically prevent serious games competing in terms of fidelity (save a few high-budget examples such as *America's Army*), the arena in which most serious games choose to compete directly with leisure games is the interaction and immersion, which can be achieved as easily through a well-designed two-dimensional web game as within a complex three-dimensional world.

Finally, there is increasing direction in the entertainment game industry towards considering serious components and overtones to games; *Wii-fit*, and *Dr. Kawashima's Brain Training*, although often disputed in terms of genuine serious outcomes (Graves et al., 2007) have demonstrated a clear appetite amongst large sections of the general public for games which encourage physical and mental well-being. It is perhaps this market which will prove most interesting in the future, as leisure game developers recognise serious elements as a way to reach wider audiences. In doing so, the convergence of state-of-the-art entertainment technology with effective and informed pedagogic design will offer the potential to create games which represent educational content in new, innovative, and imaginative ways.

AUTHOR INFO

Dr Sara de Freitas has recently taken up a new role as Director of Research at the Serious Games Institute at the University of Coventry where she leads an applied research team working closely with industry. The Institute is the first of its kind in the UK and it is envisaged that it will play a leading role in future developments of game-based learning.

Formerly Sara worked as Lab Manager, Project Manager on development programmes and Senior Research Fellow at the London Knowledge Lab. The Lab is a collaborative venture between Birkbeck College and the Institute of Education, University of London focusing upon technology assisted learning. Sara continues to hold a visiting senior research fellowship at the Lab.

Sara also works with the UK Joint Information Systems Committee e-Learning Development Programme in the Innovation strand, exploring the applications and developments of innovative technologies upon post-16 learning. Sara's recent report Learning in Immersive Worlds reviews the uses of game-based learning and presents a set of case studies of practice. Sara is also working with TruSim (Blitz Games), the Vega Group PLC and the Universities of Birmingham and Sheffield on a £2 million UK Department of Trade and Industry co-funded Serious Games research and development project which will develop highly immersive learning games to solve business training needs.

In 2003 Sara founded the UK Lab Group, which brings the research and development community together to create stronger links between industrial and academic research through supporting collaborative programmes and for showcasing innovative R&D solutions for the knowledge economy. Sara publishes in the areas of: pedagogy and e-learning; change management and strategy development for implementing e-learning systems and educational games and electronic simulations for supporting post-16 training and learning. Sara also works as a consultant through her recently established partnership company: Innovatech llp.

Professor Sara de Freitas, Ph D
Serious Games Institute
Coventry Innovation Village
Coventry University Technology Park
Cheetah Road, Coventry, CV1 2TL
West Midlands, United Kingdom
Tel: + 44 (0) 7974984351
Email: sfreitas@cad.coventry.ac.uk
Web: http://www.seriousgamesinstitute.co.uk

Dr. Ian Dunwell is a postdoctoral researcher at the Serious Games Institute, currently leading the area of games for health. Having obtained his PhD in Computer Science from the University of Hull, he also holds a degree in Physics from Imperial College London, and is an Associate of the Royal College of Science. His research interests lie primarily in the application of an understanding of cognitive processes within virtual environments as a means for providing optimised and effective learning experiences to users, and the use and evaluation of novel HCI interface technologies to enable more meaningful and affect-based interactions between humans and machines. In the domain of serious games, he has consulted with a number of leading serious game companies including Blitz Games and PlayGen to design and develop evaluation strategies for serious games such as Patient Rescue, i-Seed, and Parent Know-How, and worked extensively with games aimed at reaching difficult demographics as well as changing the affect and motivation of learners. European-funded project involvement has included defining the overarching pedagogic design for four serious games within the European-Union funded e-Vita (European Life Experiences) project, and preliminary design work towards the repurposing of medical learning objects within the mEducator consortium.

Email: IDunwell@cad.coventry.ac.uk

REFERENCES

BinSubaih, A., Maddock, S., & Romano, D. (2008). Developing a serious game for police training. *Handbook of Research on Effective Electronic Gaming in Education*, Information Science Reference

Bogost, I. (2007) *Persuasive Games – the expressive power of videogames*. Cambridge, MA: MIT Press

Chen, Y. F., Rebolledo-Mendez, G., Liarokapis, F., de Freitas, S. & Parker, E. (2008). The use of virtual world platforms for supporting an emergency response training exercise. *Proceedings of the 13th International Conference on Computer Games: AI, Animation, Mobile, Interactive Multimedia, Educational & Serious Games,* 47-55.

Csikszentmihalyi, M. (1991) *Flow: the Psychology of Optimal Experience*. New York: Harper Collins

Davidovitch, L. Parush, A., & Shtub, A. (2009). The Impact of Functional Fidelity in Simulator-based Learning of Project Management. *International Journal of Engineering Education*, 25(2), 333-340.

de Freitas, S., & Oliver, M. (2006). How can exploratory learning with games and simulations within the curriculum be most effectively evaluated? *Computers & Education*, 46, 249-264.

Graves, L., Stratton, G., Ridgers, N. D., & Cable, T., (2007). Comparison of energy expenditure in adolescents when playing new generation and sedentary computer games: cross sectional study. *British Medical Journal,* 335, 1282-1284.

Guidi, G., Frischer, B., De Simone, M., Cioci, A., Spinetti, A., Carosso, L., Loredana Micoli, L., Russo, M., & Grasso, T., (2005) "Virtualizing Ancient Rome: 3D Acquisition and Modeling of a Large Plaster-of-Paris Model of Imperial Rome," *Videometrics VIII*, 5665, 119-133.

Jackson, S., & Livingstone, I., (1982) *The Warlock of Firetop Mountain*. UK: Wizard Books

Jarvis, S., & de Freitas, S. (2009) Evaluation of an Immersive Learning Programme to Support Triage Training: In-game Feedback and its effect on Learning Transfer. *Proceedings of IEEE Games and Virtual Worlds for Serious Applications (VS-GAMES '09)*, 117-122.

Kato, P., Cole, S. W., Bradlyn, S. & Pollock, B. H. (2008) A video game improves behavioural outcomes in adolescents and young adults with cancer: a randomised trial. *Pediatrics*, 122(2), 305-317.

Knez, I., & Niedenthal, S. (2008) Lighting in digital game worlds: Effects on affect and play performance. *Cyberpsychology & Behavior*, 11, 129–137.

Kort, B., Reilly, R., Picard R. W. (2001) An Affective model of interplay between emotions and learning: reengineering educational pedagogy - building a learning companion. *Proceedings of IEEE International Conference on Advanced Learning Technologies*. 43-46.

Park, George D., & Allen, R.W. (2005) Training effectiveness: How does driving simulator fidelity influence driver performance? *Proceedings of the Human Factors and Ergonomic Society 49th Annual Meeting,* 5, 2201-2205.

Roussos, M., Johnson, A., Moher, T., Leigh, J., Vasilakis, C., & Barnes, C. (1999) Learning and Building Together in an Immersive Virtual World. *Presence: Teleoperators and Virtual Environments*. 8(3), 247-263.

Rebolledo-Mendez, G., Dunwell, I., Martinez-Miron, M., Vargas-Cerdan, M., de Freitas, S., Liarokapis, F., & Garcia-Gaona, A. (2009) Assessing Neurosky's Usability to Detect Attention Levels in an Assessment Exercise. *Proceedings of HCI International Conference*, 5610, 149-158.

Tashiro, J. S. & Dunlap, D. (2007) The impact of realism on learning engagement in educational games. *Proceedings of the 2007 Conference on Future Play (Future Play '07)*, 113-120.

Tate, R., Haritatos, J. & Cole, S. (2009) HopeLab's approach to Re-Mission. *International Journal of Learning and Media,* 1(1), 29-35.

Warburton, S. (2009). Second Life in higher education: Assessing the potential for and the barriers to deploying virtual worlds in learning and teaching, *British Journal of Educational Technology*. 40(3), 414-426.

Longhurst, P., Debattista, K., & Chalmers, A. (2006) A GPU based Saliency Map for High-Fidelity Selective Rendering. *AFRIGRAPH 2006 4th International Conference on Computer Graphics, Virtual Reality, Visualisation and Interaction in Africa*, pp. 21–29.

Zyda, M. (2005) From visual simulation to virtual reality to games. *Computer*, 28(9), 25-32.

LINKS

Act3D (*Quest3D*) *http://www.act-3d.com*
Agilingua (*ATOM Spoken Dialogue Engine) http://www.agilingua.com*
Bethesda Softworks *(Fallout 3) http://www.bethsoft.com*
Crytek (*Crysis) http:///www.crytek.com*
Coney (*A Small Town Anywhere*) *http://www.youhavefoundconey.net*
Google (*Google Earth*) *http://earth.google.com*
HopeLab (*Re-mission) http://www.hopelab.org*
Nintendo (*Wii-Fit, Dr. Kawashima's Brain Training*) *http://www.nintendo.com*
Oil Productions (*Sneeze*) *http://www.c2h6.com/*
Rockstar Games (*Grand Theft Auto*) *http://www.rockstargames.com*
Selex Systems Integration (*Ward Off Infection*) *http://www.selexsi.co.uk*
TruSim (*Triage Trainer, Patient Rescue*) *http://www.trusim.com*
Valve Software (*Half-Life) http://www.valvesoftware.com*
Wikimedia Foundation (*GeoWiki*) *http://wikimediafoundation.org/wiki*

In: Interactive and Digital Media for Education in Virtual … ISBN: 978-1-61668-844-8
Editor: Cai Yiyu

Chapter 6

3D Visibility Analysis in Virtual Learning Environments and Interactive and Digital Media

Arthur van Bilsen
Faculty of Technology, Policy and Management,
Delft University of Technology, The Netherlands

Abstract

The author describes the potential of 3D visibility analysis (VA) in Virtual Learning Environments (VLE) and Interactive & Digital Media (IDM). With a focus on Serious Games (a type of IDM), a context of education and serious gaming in the Netherlands is provided. The potential of VA for education through VLE and IDM is found in increased support for the design of the game world and the desired behaviors that occur within it. As human perception occurs real time in a 3D world, 3D visibility analysis is needed to realize this support. The application of 3D visibility analysis is exemplified by connecting visual measures, via game world design, to learning goals in a training simulation game.

Introduction

Education is in a process of profound change internationally, as are the tools which aim to support it. Virtual learning environments (VLEs) are on the rise and increasingly enable visitors to engage in three-dimensional space. As three-dimensional worlds have become common in the entertainment game industry, expectations of spaces in interactive and digital media (IDM) are equally high. On the other hand, the tools to analyze three-dimensional worlds are struggling to cope with the developments. The author introduces three-dimensional visibility analysis (3DVA) as a theoretical and practical method (Van Bilsen, 2008) to meet with the expectations. Visibility analysis encompasses a set of techniques and concepts for analyzing visibility aspects of real or virtual environments. The goal of this chapter is to describe and explore the possibilities of 3DVA, for supporting spatial VLEs within IDM. Educational learning goals are expected to be better accommodated if the design and behavior of spatial VLEs is supported by 3DVA. The case study presented provides some evidence in favor of such a claim.

Firstly, I elaborate on VLEs and simulation games in education, and provide some typical examples from the Netherlands. Secondly, I focus on the tools that support spatial VLEs and show how 3D visibility analysis can improve the virtual world's behavior and design. For example, path planning and safety issues are being related to visibility analysis. Finally, I conclude with a summary of the arguments and observations.

Within the spectrum of IDM—a broad term—the focus in this chapter is on VLEs and simulation games. With VLEs I mean virtual worlds with a learning goal. Of particular interest with regard to 3DVA will be simulation games with a *spatial* game world, in which players and agents walk around and act (first person view) or in which a spatial physical structure is to be designed, such as in SimCity (third person overview).

Education in the Netherlands

In the past decade, education in the Netherlands has seen a number of transformations that frame the recent developments towards serious gaming. In higher education, the Anglo-Saxon model of Bachelors and Masters has been implemented, lining up existing courses with international standards. Higher education in the Netherlands aims to lead students to a professional or academic level. But instead of 'learning for life', young people are increasingly expected to embrace 'life-long learning' (Education Council, 2003). As a result, institutions in the Netherlands are also involved in post-academic education and in-company training.

With regard to K-12, government policy has shifted from a traditional educational model towards a more progressive model called *the new learning*. Over longer periods of time, both extremes are seen to have advantages and drawbacks. The advantages of traditional education are the support for theoretic and analytic thinking, factual knowledge and individual performance. The drawbacks are considered to be the occurrence of mindless repetition, reproduction without insight, and lack of motivation. The proponents of *the new learning* emphasize the development of resourcefulness, social and communicative skills and autonomy, while the opponents point to the lack of factual knowledge, negotiable assessment and performance, and strategic behavior of students working in groups.

I will not go into the details of the *pros* and *cons* of these models, but observe that they are in a perpetual cycle in time. The cycle persists as overemphasis of the drawbacks of one model leads to the adoption of the opposite model. Subsequently, overemphasis of the caveats of the new model, stirs rebellion back towards the first model (Prensky, 2001; Gee, 2003). Serious gaming is not part of either camp. To break out of the cycle, dug in positions are to be swapped for balanced arguments. A middle ground is to be sought, where the best of both worlds is combined, while preventing the drawbacks of their extremes. Interestingly, in this process gaming can play a supporting role in both contexts sketched above, as is explored by Mayer, Stegers-Jager and Bekebrede (2007: 56-62). Computer games are a typical and well known type of interactive and digital media (IDM). The developments in education have put higher demands on the quality of educational computer games. Games will therefore benefit from more informed behavioral models, such as those supported by visibility analysis. In the next section, the wide range of further applications of computer games is elaborated on.

SERIOUS GAMES: INTERACTIVE AND DIGITAL MEDIA FOR EDUCATION

Ever since the early 1950s, games have been purposefully applied in education. At first the classrooms are occasionally filled by analog games such as card games, board games, puzzles, role-play games, social simulations, *etc.* (Greenblat and Duke, 1975). Claims about the effects of games include: increased motivation for a topic, increased cognitive learning, enriched educational environment, improved skills, change of attitude, increased self evaluation and increased participation (Greenblat, 1975, 1988). In the late 1960s, computer simulation models are introduced to support mostly the calculation of results, used as feed back to player decisions. But, the added value was limited or even impeded learning (Duke, 2000), as simulation technology and human computer interaction were still premature. Even in as late as the 1990s, the introduction of gaming in the K-12 segment in the USA ended in failure (Salen and Zimmerman, 2004).

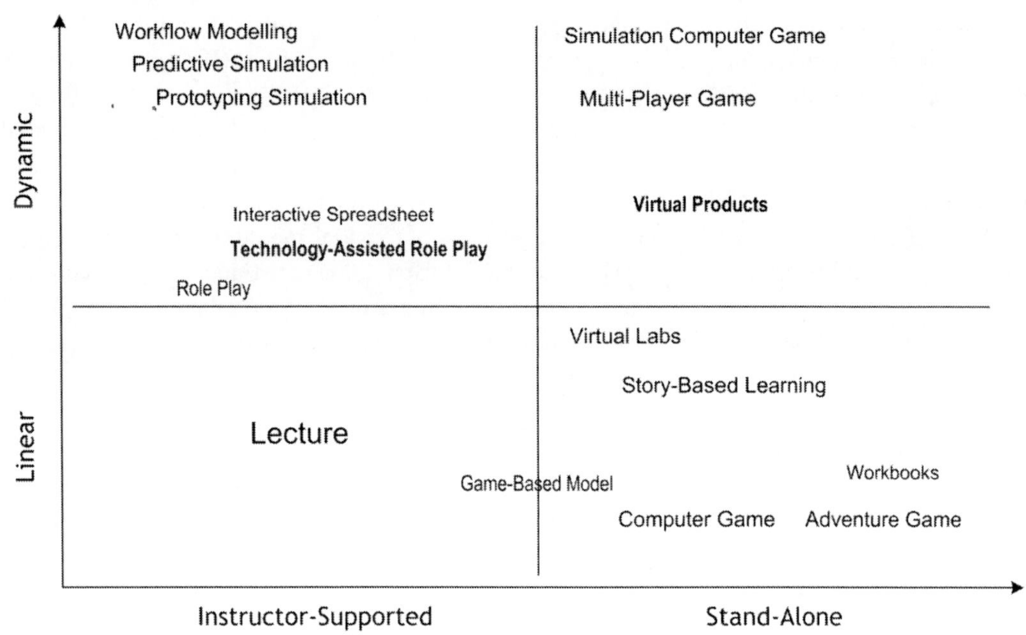

Figure 1. Educational Simulations and Tangential Spaces. The figure shows a selection from (Aldrich, 2005, p.64).

Only since the late 1990s the overall picture changes from edutainment to serious gaming, mainly due to the popularity of entertainment games. Games are found useful for arriving at a complete view of a given issue (Duke and Geurts, 2004) and for integrating different perspectives and disciplines (Kriz, 2003). For example by switching roles, players can adapt and learn to understand different perspectives, experience the system from different angles, and learn from these differences (Duke and Geurts, 2004). The number of game types expands revolutionarily and new types keep emerging to the present day. These are shown together with traditional types of educational means in Figure 1.

One of many possible examples of a new type is the Global Supply Chain Game. Viewed in terms of Aldrich's diagram (Figure 1) it is an interactive spreadsheet, a simulation computer game and a multiplayer game. The new generation of simulation games does not only bring new technology, but also new ways of support for learning (Gee, 2003; Aldrich, 2005). In the meantime, the number of application domains of simulation games is growing: healthcare, defense, environment, politics and education (Michael and Chen, 2006). Games and VLEs from some of these domains from the Netherlands are elaborated on in the next section.

Simulation Games and Virtual Learning Environments in the Netherlands

Commercial virtual worlds, such as World of Warcraft and EVE Online, are still far ahead of their serious counterparts when it comes to technology, graphics, ease of use and popularity. But *serious* applications are catching up, reusing both the technology (*e.g.* game engines) and learning support methods (*e.g.* tutorials, forums). In this section I will elaborate on simulation games and VLEs, as interactive and digital media (IDM), which were developed in the Netherlands.

Research and studies about computer games in Dutch education show there is a potential for gaming in education, but that improvement is necessary. There are two main alternatives for a new approach (Van Eck, 2006): 1) The use of repurposed commercial off the shelf (COTS) games, such as using SimCity for lessons about spatial planning or Civilization III for lessons about history (Squire, 2004; Egenfeldt-Nielsen, 2005); 2) Educators, students and game developers can join to create new games revolving around certain themes, exemplified amply by Social Impact Games (Prensky, 2007). Both approaches have their up and down sides, see Egenfeldt-Nielsen (2004) for more details, but in general still act as thresholds for educators.

Nevertheless, learning environments with educational value are being developed in the mobility, safety and healthcare sectors. Although there are many examples of VLEs from the Netherlands, the following cases are selected for their inclusion of a spatial three-dimensional environment. The fulfillment of educational goals can potentially benefit from 3D visibility analysis, as we will see in the next section.

In the mobility sector one finds the case of *Ship Simulator* by VSTEP, originally intended as a serious game, but now available commercially. It is used by the MCAST Maritime Institute for educational purposes, but also attracts simulation and sailing fans. The game has accurate handling and physics, but for the commercial market, it also needed appealing graphics. This has resulted in a simulation game with a highly realistic 3D virtual world, comparable to entertainment games and at a very acceptable cost for education.

In the safety sector, Artesis Virtual and VSTEP developed *Virtuele Brandweer Trainingen* (Virtual Firefighter Training). This simulation is used in firefighter education. The player walks around with a first person perspective in a realistic 3D virtual world, while the instructor has an overview and is able to introduce events in real time. After the training, the built-in replay facility supports learning during the debriefing.

In the healthcare sector, Delltatech developed *Simendo*, a simulator for endoscopy. Simendo is played by surgeons-to-be during their education. The focus is not on surgery but on the development of more general hand-eye coordination skills. The player is asked to perform tasks such as to build a tower of blocks or make a knot, by using exact copies of real endoscopic equipment. The equipment is connected to a laptop showing the 3D view of the virtual world, in which the blocks and threads reside. Incentives to play are stimulated by an online list of top scores.

With regard to education, games and VLEs fit for *both* professionals and students are of extra value. Students are the managers and professionals of the future. An example is the Dutch simulation game SimPort which has been played extensively by both professionals and students (Bekebrede and Mayer, 2006). In SimPort, players plan and build an extension of the port of Rotterdam, the Netherlands. During the game, the players interact with a 3D world, in which the plan comes to life via a third person perspective. Simulation games such as SimPort represent complex socio-technical systems, in which players are found to learn specifically about the in-game case (Van Bilsen, Bekebrede and Mayer, 2010). Another professional training game in first person view is *Dijkpatrouille* (Levee Patroller) by Deltares and Delft University of Technology, which aims to train levee patrollers. Where real life scenario training of bursting levees is costly, the game allows for flexible scenarios to be built and played in a 3D virtual world. During the game, visibility plays a role as players need to visually spot, reach and analyze "failures" in and around levees.

One can observe that serious games and virtual learning environments are becoming more and more common in the Netherlands and internationally. The tools to design, build and analyze games evolve accordingly. When looking more closely at the examples above one can identify situations where visibility analysis can potentially play a significant role. The range from 'game character behavior' to the 'possibility of finding levee failures', can be related to visibility, visibility-based intelligence, vision and proximity. In the remainder of this chapter the potential role of 3D visibility analysis in IDM and VLEs is explored in a more general sense, and exemplified with a case.

Serious Games and 3D Visibility Analysis

Simulation games or serious games can generally be defined as experiential, rule-based but open environments where players learn by taking actions and experiencing the effects through feedback mechanisms in and around the game. The underlying idea is that the individual and social learning in the game can be transferred to the outside world, but that the actions in the game have no undesirable or immediate impact on reality (Mayer & Veeneman, 2002; Duke 1974, 1980).

In an educational context learning is desired and computer games enable this through the experience of a virtual world. The majority of information contributing to the experiential nature of games comes from sight. Apart from sound and force feedback, the effects of actions in the game world are fed back to the player by visual means.

Figure 2. A screenshot from 'first person shooter' HalfLife 2 (Valve, 2004).

The relation between 3DVA (Van Bilsen, 2008) and gaming is rooted in a key aspect of the human interaction process, namely the visual interaction. Neglecting the other senses, the visual input (*e.g.* everything on the screen) results in a response from the player. In most computer games this immediately results in a visual response from the game or the other players. As this cycle iterates continuously, vision is evidently seen to be at the heart of the digital gaming process (role I below). As vision occurs in 3D space and time, only a 3DVA method (*ibid.*) is able to support this visual interaction cycle closely.

Outside computer games, vision is obviously of more general use for sighted people. Vision is used to move around, to facilitate collision anticipation, vision is the dominant sense, the richest source of information, and facilitates the use of objects in the environment. These processes also occur in games, while players are immersed through visual interaction, such as exemplified in Figure 2.

Vision, Player and Gaming

In Figure 3 the position of visual information in a larger scheme is shown. The iterative cycle contains a simulation game and the player or agent. The simulation game (upper right) poses challenges and visual input to the player, which feeds the subtle processes of perception (Biederman, 1993; Marr, 1982) and conception. Subsequently, the player combines perception and conception with short term and long term memory to come to actions and skill improvement (Figure 3, lower right). The "optimal" functioning of this loop is found when the player reaches a state of flow (Csíkszentmihályi, 1990), where learning (right horizontal axis) is achieved by an adapted interplay between challenges and skills (upper right). It must be noted that immersion depends not just on vision and may in general also depend on sound or other sensorial inputs.

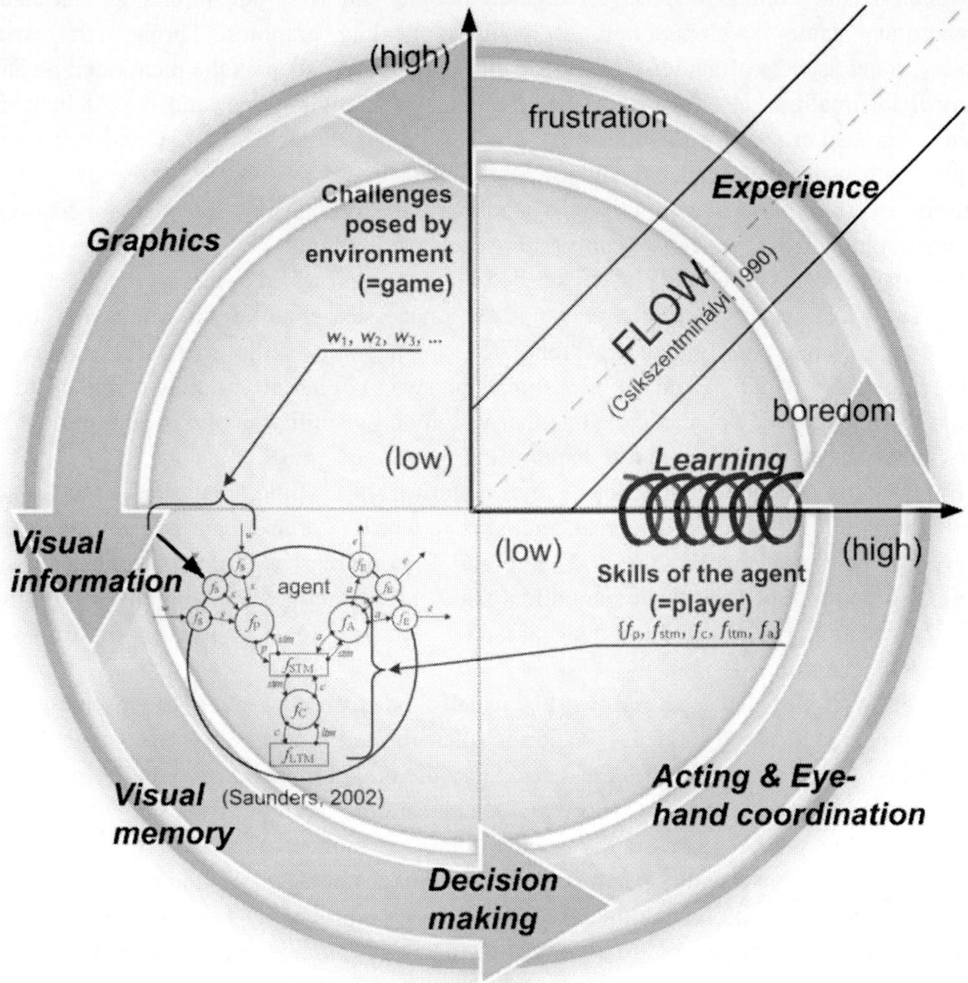

Figure 3. The player-game interaction (PGI) cycle connects the player agent to learning and flow through vision (Van Bilsen, 2009).

Looking closer, two main aspects can be observed in the gaming process where vision and visibility play an important role:

I. In the visual interaction between the player and the game or the other players (as described above). This is referred to as 'vision'.
II. In the vision-based intelligence of opponents and the related design of the game world and its internal simulation.

The game world itself (II) plays an important role, as the *place and time* of the action. The working of the game world depends on the designer's intentions (*e.g.* fantasy, sci-fi, realism), but generally shows a consistent set of rules, such as the laws of physics. Based on visual input, the player subsequently constructs an internal mental representation of the game world in memory (Figure 3, lower left), to which meaning is attached. Hence, the meaning and working of the game world result in an experience.

Vision is the dominant sense for sighted people and it is not surprising that many contemporary game developers aim at having appealing graphics. Through the years, however, other aspects of games have also gained popularity, such as the mentioned physics and artificial intelligence (AI) in a game. Design of the environment and the AI behavior within it, are also crucial for the interactive process players are involved in. Computer agents bumping into walls or taking unrealistic paths will decrease the player's sense of realism. Similarly, overly simple or complicated spatial virtual environments intended for learning, can obstruct immersion, which is a contributing factor to learning.

Immersion occurs when the player experiences the virtual world as almost real, or accepts it as "a reality". However, inversely realism is not a necessary condition for immersion. In the flow of the game, the player is stimulated to develop skills to fulfill challenges (Csíkszentmihályi, 1990). From an educational perspective, a state of flow is linked to an optimal learning curve. One can conclude that vision and visibility analysis are important for games in two ways: through both role I and role II mentioned above.

But how can education and serious games benefit from visibility analysis? Let us look at some examples that apply to the real and virtual world. For example *privacy*, which is achieved at points in space with good view and low angular exposure, may just as well benefit a sniper opponent in a war simulation game, who benefits from both cover and view. Similarly, remaining undetected is a goal shared by both a thief and a special agent team on a hostage rescue mission.

Games with populated virtual worlds usually have some kind of agent model. In computational agent-based modeling, vision is often limited to a small set of distances from other agents and objects, which are pre-selected by the model maker. Using the full spectrum of visibility characteristics one can more realistically mimic the input from the environment. And one needs to make fewer assumptions about the environment, allowing for more detailed measurements and consequently potentially more sophisticated agents and improved learning.

With regard to artificial intelligence, 3DVA can improve the behavior of intelligent opponents, which players expect to be aware of their environment and its dynamics. On the design side, 3D VLEs can only be adequately supported by an analysis method that is also 3D. For both design and behavior of 3D worlds, visibility measures are suggested in a later section. First, the current status of VA in relation to past achievements and empirical data (next section) and the used visibility analysis method are elaborated on.

ACHIEVEMENTS AND EMPIRICAL DATA OF VA

The claims of the potential of VA for real and virtual worlds ought to be based in past achievements and empirical data. The achievements of Space Syntax (Hillier and Hanson, 1984; Hillier, 1997) in horizontal 2D with a relatively simple method, can be explained partially by two characteristics of the visual system: the tendency to try and avoid collisions while moving, and a limited memory or knowledge of the environment, which prevents *e.g.* explorative shoppers from deviating more than 2 or 3 turns from the main streets. Potential collisions occur almost always in the horizontal directions, where also most of the interesting physical objects are found.

However, apart from exploration, human agents try to understand their environment (Kaplan and Kaplan 1989), and a 2D approach is insufficient. Understanding the environment starts with sensorial input, via perception, to conception through the interaction with memory as noted before (see the agent model in Figure 3). The dominant visual input consists of a projection of the three-dimensional environment on the retina. Thus understanding starts with at least the three-dimensional environment, where time (change of the retinal image), as the fourth dimension, plays a crucial role in 'seeing'. Not only does the retina cease to transfer a 100% static image after 2-3 seconds (Yarbus, 1967), seeing and perceiving also includes walking around objects, which takes time (Gibson, 1987). Through perception and conception, the input is used to perform actions that produce effects in the outside world, such as the navigation and manipulation of objects.

Visual estimation of distances is particularly important in navigating through crowds. Dynamic simulations of crowds have been conducted in 2D and semi-3D with limited visibility characteristics and reasonable to good predictive value (Batty *et al.* 2003; Hoogendoorn and Daamen, 2007). Stamps (2005) gives a broad overview of empirical research relating the geometrical aspects of space to the experience of space. Visual permeability, locomotive permeability and enclosure of a pedestrian's environment are found to correlate with judgements on safety. Neurophysiologic findings indicate that there is a region in the brain that responds strongly to spatial enclosure (Parahippocampal Place Area - PPA; Epstein and Kanwisher 1998). Other research shows significant correlation between principal lines of sight (called axial lines) and pedestrian movement (Hillier 1998; Carvalho and Batty 2003). Correlations have also been found between perceived openness and multiple isovist measures (Franz and Wiener 2005). More recently, visibility analysis was used to provide a quantifiable basis for Kevin Lynch's urban analysis (Lynch, 1960), an example of refining and extending a seminal work in urban design (Morello and Ratti, 2009).

With regard to applications one finds examples in several distinct fields such as economy, archaeology, ecology and criminology. From an economic perspective, there is a correlation between visibility and location value. In studying archaeological sites, visibility analysis is used for reconstructing past pedestrian movement patterns (O'Sullivan and Turner 2001). In ecology, visibility analysis is used for the improvement and design of animal habitats. Visibility analysis has also been refined to aid crime prevention, linking criminology to urban design (Newman 1972; Nes 2005). Visibility is connected to human beings, who naturally tend *not* to act or think in separate disciplines such as those mentioned. An opportunity for visibility analysis is found in the use of common concepts across these visibility-related disciplines. Serious gaming in particular, is one of the areas where the human factor is crucial, and therefore exploring the possible contributions of visibility analysis is of interest.

3DVA Method

While VLEs with *spatial* worlds become increasingly common in education, the tools to analyze them are largely still premature. To ensure learning goals are met, proper analysis is needed to support the design of physical and behavioral aspects of VLEs. Both interior and exterior environments occur in VLEs, as can be observed from the examples in later sections.

In this section, a 3DVA method is described. It extends existing methods for the analysis and design of built environments, found in architectural and urban design.

The used mathematical framework for 3DVA in this chapter, builds on Benedikt's framework. In line with Batty (2001, p.124), the first step is not to summarize space as do Peponis, Wineman, Bafna, Rashid, Hong Kim and Bafna (1998a; 1998b, 1997), but to work with the full visual field at each vantage point. The mathematical foundation for visibility analyses was laid by Benedikt (1979) and with the extension by Van Bilsen (2008) was coined Isovist-based Visibility Analysis (IBVA). An isovist is defined (non-mathematicaly) as 'all space visible from a vantage point', where space and isovist can be two or three-dimensional (Figure 4).

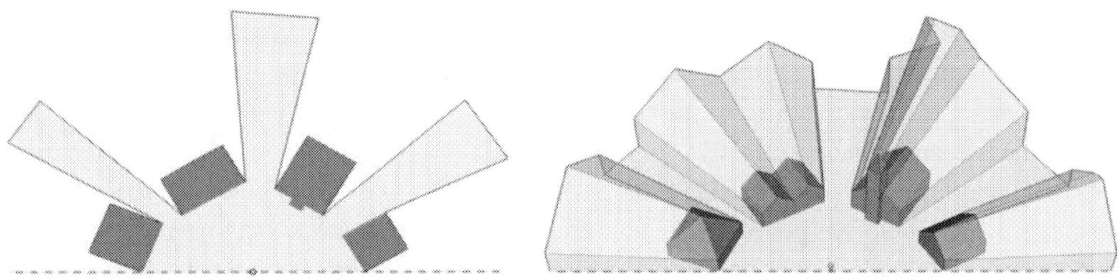

Figure 4. On the left, a 2D isovist (shaded) in a 2D world. On the right, a 3D isovist (shaded *boundary*) in a 3D world. From: Van Bilsen and Stolk (2007).

Mathematically, an isovist is defined as a connected region of points visible to a given vantage point. In IBVA an isovist is defined further as a function, that returns radial distances, facilitating theory development, isovist generation and measure calculation. The radial distance depends on the direction (θ, φ) the light arrives from, shown in Figure 5 (right).

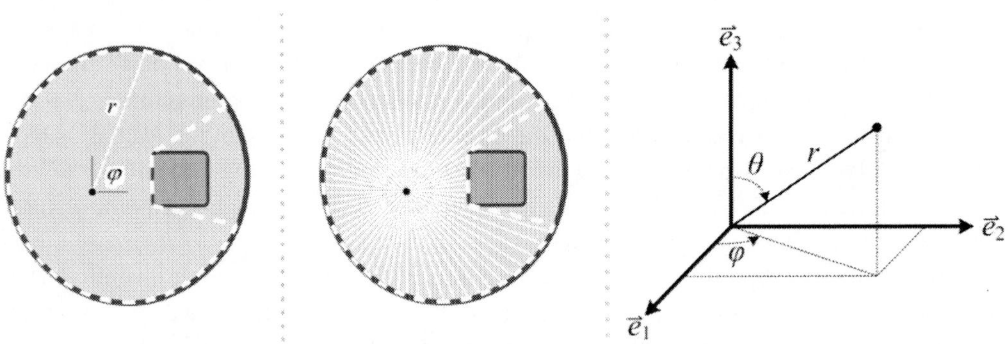

Figure 5. The isovist defined as a set of radial distances from a vantage point in 2D (left and center) and 3D (right), where the observer resides at the origin. From Van Bilsen (2008).

Nevertheless, the actual calculation of 3D visibility measures in practical applications remained a hard problem. Early applications were for the majority conducted on a 2D map and this is still the dominant use today. However, according to Morello and Ratti (2009, p.1): "Traditional calculation methods consider a model which is too far from real human visual experience: first, it does not take into account the vertical dimension of the analyzed space is 2D; second, traditional methods do not consider the dynamic participation of moving through space, which is a fundamental characteristic of visual knowledge". The behavior of human and automated agents in architectural and urban environments is not fully analyzable through 2D models and 2D isovists, as vision occurs in 3D space. Finally, 2D tools do not use the full potential of VA, since the design of real and virtual worlds already takes place in 3D CAD environments.

In the development of 3D measures, first steps have been taken: *spatial openness* by Fisher-Gewirtzmann and Wagner (2003), *sky opening* by Teller (2003), real world measurements of the latter by Sarradin (2004) and more recently various measures in digital elevation models (DEMs) by Morello and Ratti (2009). However none of these can be considered a general three-dimensional approach. For example, DEMs cannot adequately represent cities when it comes to observer experience of inside spaces (roofed) and outside spaces (arches, bridges, etc.). Technology used for entertainment games is improving at an exponential rate. This technology is used by the author to obtain large amounts of visibility information on acceptable timescales: full three-dimensional analyses have become feasible[1] (Van Bilsen, 2008, 2009). Similar approaches are found in military research and applications. The calculation power of the graphics buffer is used for studying synthetic perception and target detection (Darken, 2007). The resulting data (the set of radial distances to the environment) can be used for scientific analysis, since it is both quantitative and amenable to error analysis (Van Bilsen and Stolk, 2008). Some of the first results can support the analysis of virtual game worlds in new ways and an example from a serious game environment is elaborated on in section *Example of Supervisor* below.

The added value of three-dimensional analysis as compared to two-dimensional analysis is summarized in the following (non-exhaustive) list of points (Van Bilsen, 2009):

a. The vertical dimension (*e.g.* building height) is ignored in 2D and therefore its influence on visibility measures;
b. Walkable surfaces of cities differ in height, such as on hills and bridges;
c. Incomplete landmark analysis in 2D, if any;
d. Facade analysis, the (inter)visibility between facades with regard to privacy, is possible in 3D;
e. The possibility to relate to concepts relevant to urban design and planning like building density and incidence of sunlight, which are based on 3D measures;
f. Comparison of perspectives with regard to safety (*e.g.* adult and child);
g. A typology of space based on the full 3D environment;
h. A connection to cognitive pattern recognition, which occurs in 3D;
i. Discrimination of lighting and cover conditions during night and day, bad and good weather, for navigation and safety.

I will not go into these points here, but it is clear that 3DVA analyses open up a new world of opportunities for theoretical and practical applications. It is argued that the points apply to the analysis of the real world as well as for game worlds. Game worlds have started to approach the real world in various ways. Not in the least because consumers desire ever more immersive, interactive, open, graphically appealing, realistic and complex virtual environments. As analysis methods have progressed to 3D, visibility analysis can now support learning in spatial VLEs through 3DVA indicators.

---

[1] The software used for the analyses in this chapter was provided by Aisophyst.

3DVA INDICATORS

As is evident from the isovists in Figure 4 and Figure 5, the number of possible measures—based on the full set of radial distances from a single vantagepoint—is vast. In our terminology, measures or combinations thereof, are possible indicators for something. An overview of measures is presented by Van Bilsen (2008) in which the mathematical definitions of those presented below can be found. In the following, a selection of basic visibility measures and what they may indicate, is presented. Note that, depending on one's educational learning goals, some measures will be more appropriate in supporting the design of a virtual learning environment than others.

Using the Aisophyst software, provided generation of the 3D isovist fields in Figure 6 and Figure 7, with which little over 1.5 million radials were generated and traversed at each vantage point, with an average of $8 \cdot 10^{-6}$ steradian per radial.

Proximity and particularly the detection of collisions are ubiquitous (Cai *et al*, 2006). Other applications require the prevention of collisions. The closest object to the observer is pointed at by the isovist's minimum radius, *MINR* (see Figure 9 for an example). From the MINR-field the "safest" path is obtained by taking the spatial derivative. This path leads pedestrians farthest from obstacles they can potentially collide with and is equivalent to the Voronoi diagram.

The average distance to the environment, *AVGR-3D*, is a good indicator for the amount of accessible volume around an observer (Figure 6, left). Volume may indicate both available distance as well as visible area (orthogonal to radials) and does not discriminate between the two. If the variance is low, AVGR-3D provides a sense of the openness and overview in an environment. The measure AVGR-3D is also the first in a range of parameters that can classify an environment according to the isovist's spectrum.

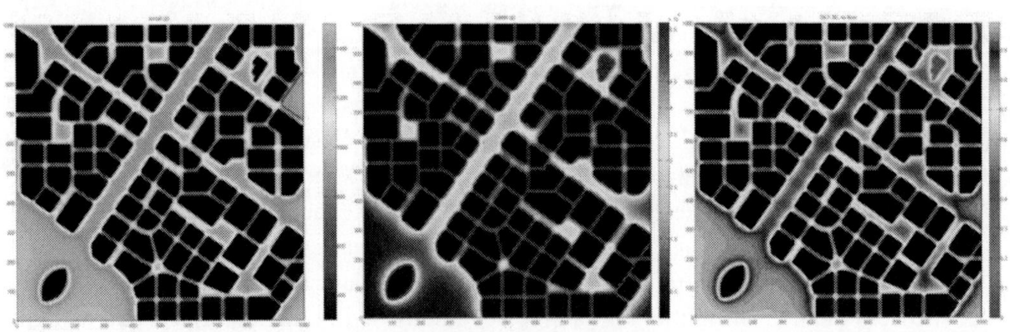

Figure 6. Three 3D isovist measures in a fictional 1 km x 1 km neighborhood: average radial distance (left, AVGR-3D), variance in the radial distance (center, VARR-3D) and the sky opening factor or the solid angle of sky visible (right, SKY-3D).

Similar to AVGR-3D, the variance *VARR-3D* shows a smooth field that indicates the diversity in the depth field (Figure 6 center and Figure 7). The perimeter in the horizontal plane *PER-2D*, provides a more detailed indication of places with high information load (Figure 7). The 'gradient of the PER-2D'-field indicates potential surprise at points where new information becomes available (*e.g.* when crossing the lines in Figure 7). Van Bilsen and Poelman (2009) argue in the context of a training game that people visiting a site for the first time, will need time to take in the complexity of the structure. They may stand still suddenly or have less attention for dangerous situations developing in their proximity. From a learning and training perspective, information overload is usually best avoided, and a more gradual introduction of information in space and time is preferable. For virtual learning environment designers, these indicators can support finding a suitable information load and hence a desired learning curve.

The measure *SKY-3D* provides the amount of sky visible to a particular observation point, measured in steradians (Figure 6, right). Consequently, it also indicates at the potential of natural light arriving at a point and may contribute to the feeling of openness of the environment. Lighting conditions are important for all kinds of workplaces and are embedded in law in many countries. In public space light is important for both safety and leisure activities. As the sky is also the source of various hostile weather conditions such as snow, rain and wind, the measure is also an indicator of the absence of shelter against these conditions. In this manner, the design of both shelter and an efficient lighting distribution may be aided by the SKY-3D isovist field (Van Bilsen and Poelman, 2009).

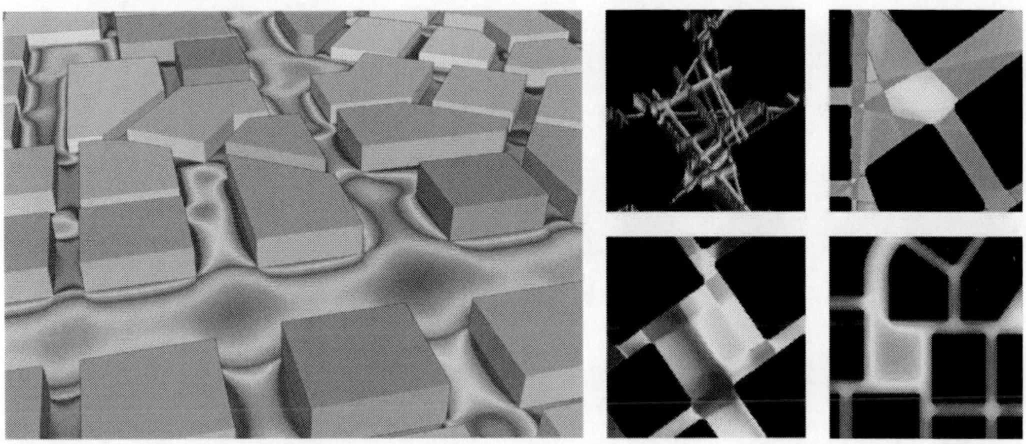

Figure 7. Left: a perspective view of the calculation plane of AVGR-3D (average radial distance) in the 3D environment. Right, clockwise (start upper left): gradient of PER-2D (perimeter), PER-2D, VARR-3D (variance) and AREA-2D.

In Figure 7 and Figure 8 also 2D measures are shown with on average 0.18 degree per radial (or 2044 radials per 360 degrees). Because of their sensitivity to the sharp edges in the environment, the perimeter and area in the horizontal plane clearly show different regions within an urban square (PER-2D and AREA-2D, Figure 7). Apart from surprise, the 'gradient of the perimeter' field also indicates the—theoretically relevant—epsilon spaces of Peponis *et al.* (1997).

We have scratched the surface of some of the isovist measures that indicate to important values for the design of VLEs and the modeling of intelligent behavior within them. In the next section some more measures are elaborated on in the context of an actual VLE for training personnel on an oil drilling site.

EXAMPLE OF SUPERVISOR

Supervisor is an educational training simulation built for a major international oil company. The aim is to train personnel to work safely in an oil drilling site. The virtual site in Supervisor was accurately modeled after a real drilling site (Figure 8, upper left and right). The whole VLE also includes the training of safety-related issues such as the briefing, planning and using the right clothing and equipment. In applying IBVA to the virtual world of Supervisor we try to relate quantitative 3D visibility measures to safety issues. To the author's best knowledge this is the first case of a VLE being analyzed with 3D isovist-based visibility measures. A more elaborate study of Supervisor is described by Van Bilsen and Poelman (2009).

One of the main safety issues is *movement* of objects (*e.g.* cranes, trucks) and people. Distracted or running people may not be able to prevent collisions with low obstructions or obstructions hanging from above. The dangers are shown by subtracting the two horizontal proximity fields: $S = \text{MINR-2D}^{160cm} - \text{MINR-2D}^{20cm}$ at different heights.

Figure 8. Above left: a first person view, showing cables (A), pipes (B) and stairs (C). Above right: a view of the Supervisor world as it is analyzed. Below: the isovist measure S (left) and gradient of S (right), where $S = \text{MINR-2D}^{160cm} - \text{MINR-2D}^{20cm}$. From: Van Bilsen and Poelman (2009).

Regions with more proximity at 160cm than at 20cm have positive values, of which a subset is painted white (see legend). Places where there is more proximity at 20cm than at 160cm have negative values, of which a subset is painted black. The white areas, excluding Figure 8's outer boundary line, indicate danger of tripping over obstacles. The black areas indicate where one is in danger of banging one's upper body or head, such as the stairs shown in Figure 8 (C).

Some of the black areas represent places where steel cables for stabilizing the drill tower, are pinned in the ground (A). A careless pedestrian could easily run into such a cable. Nearby white areas (below and left of A) indicate the pins used to mark the cables. The pipe storage (B) is surrounded by a white boundary that indicates tripping danger. The gradient of the subtraction S in Figure 8 (lower right), shows where the difference between heights occurs most sudden. This consequently highlights dangerous spots, where collisions, tripping and bumping may lead to serious accidents. A drawback of using planes at two heights is that a potentially dangerous pipe at 60 cm height is missed by the analysis. The 3D version of MINR at 160cm, shows the proximity of all obstacles and is shown in Figure 9. For reference, a black line marks an object's intersection with a 1 meter radius sphere around the observation point at 160 cm.

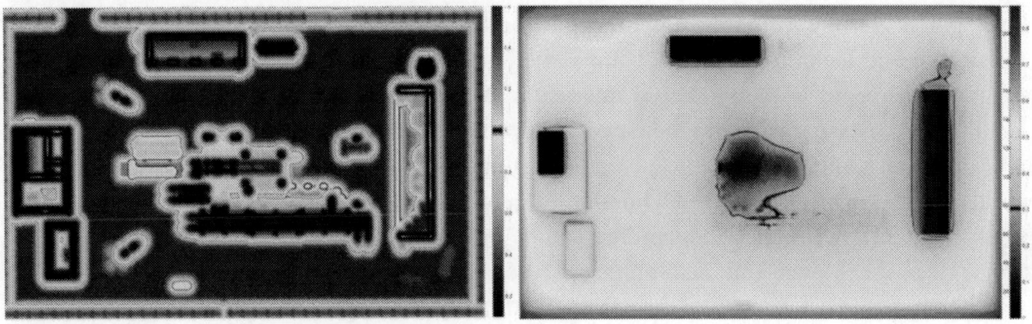

Figure 9. Left: the isovist measure MINR-3D. The black line marks intersection with a 1 meter proximity sphere. Right: the isovist measure SKY-3D. The black line encloses places with low natural lighting. Both calculation planes reside at 160 cm above the ground. From: Van Bilsen and Poelman (2009).

The blue or clouded sky and the sun provide natural lighting. The isovist measure SKY-3D (Figure 9, right) does not discriminate between these, but provides the amount of sky visible to a particular observation point, measured in steradians. In Figure 9 (right) the black line separates regions where more and less than 60% of the sky's halfsphere is visible (30% of the whole sphere). Within the black lines, the darker areas have poorer natural lighting conditions and are candidates for artificial lighting. But the sky is also the source of various hostile weather conditions such as snow, rain and wind. Hence, the inverse of SKY-3D is also an indicator of the presence of shelter. In short, the SKY-3D isovist field can aid the design of both shelter facilities and an efficient lighting distribution.

Other measures revealed the best places for a supervisor (Van Bilsen and Poelman, 2009). Supervisors need places with optimal overview, which are indicated by high AREA-2D and high AVGR-3D. With similar measures, the placement of safety equipment can be optimized. Based on AVGR-3D and MINR-2D^{20cm} three suitable locations for the so-called 'monster spot' were identified: a place outside large enough for meetings to be held and workers to be counted. With these links, we have identified some relations between quantitative 3DVA measures and safety issues within the Supervisor training simulation. Hence, the measures can potentially improve the educational learning goals of the training. It must be noted that, since this presumably is the first 3D isovist-based visibility analysis of a VLE, it is expected that new and more suitable measures will be developed in the course of time.

Conclusion

The goal of this chapter is to describe and explore the possibilities of three-dimensional visibility analysis, for supporting VLEs within IDM. By doing so it is expected that educational learning goals can be better accommodated, when the design and behavior of VLEs is quantitatively supported by 3DVA.

Three-dimensional visibility analysis holds both large opportunities and challenges for supporting spatial VLEs. The design of VLEs and the design support tools constitute a two-way relation. While education is in a process of change internationally, VLEs are on the rise and have become 3D and interactive. The support tools must match this dynamic development. Of the available support tools and methods, 3D visibility analysis matches the substantive and technical aspects of this development and supports VLE design on multiple points. With regard to the increased interaction in VLEs, it is shown that vision is a crucial part of the player-game interaction cycle, of which learning is the main goal. The 3DVA indicators are found to be able to potentially support both the design and behavior of virtual worlds. With regard to recent 3D simulation game worlds, the aspects of safety, navigation, perception, design, training and learning can be quantitatively supported by 3DVA indicators. Although past achievements and empirical research in 2D visibility analysis have paved the way, it is noted that for some of the 3D applications more empirical verification is needed. In other cases, such as with perception and conception, the disciplines themselves have yet to come to accepted theories.

In the second half of the chapter, the support for VLEs is made concrete by presenting direct relations between common issues in VLEs and quantitative 3D visibility measures. In the more general setting of a fictional neighborhood proximity-related issues such as collision detection and prevention, and visibility-related issues such as perceived openness, diversity, information overload, lighting and weather conditions and surprise, are described. In the context of an actual VLE of the simulation training game Supervisor, these issues are further elaborated on in the light of safety. The results look promising and form a basis for further research.

Outlook

The research may develop in several future directions. In any case, the visibility analysis of spatial environments yields a vast amount of data, which may contain support or falsification for existing and future hypotheses. Which hypotheses can be tested remains an open question. Nevertheless, visibility is a general notion which can work as a connecting concept across soft and hard disciplines.

The potential of 3DVA as an analysis method for the visual field in VLE and serious games is promising. The outlook on future research includes possible application in the fields of spatial cognition, agent-based modeling, genetic algorithms and traffic modeling, for example with the aim of generating design alternatives for serious game worlds, architecture, urban design and landscape architecture. On the other hand, isovist measures can help explain the behavior of real humans, by quantifying and correlating the characteristics of the space they live in. As a consequence 3DVA may also support behavior modeling of artificial agents in virtual environments, such as actors, opponents, and robots. Beside the theoretical framework and simulations, empirical verification for the 3D measures, based on real people in real environments is seen as a necessary step for VA to mature. With these developments and their advanced future tools, VLEs and serious games will be able to support learning objectives in unprecedented ways.

ACKNOWLEDGMENT

The author would like to thank Egbert Stolk, Ronald Poelman and Igor Mayer for ideas, literature, pictures, designs and models used in this chapter. The 3D visibility analysis software was provided by Aisophyst (www.aisophyst.com).

AUTHOR INFO

Arthur van Bilsen (PhD) does research in Simulation & Gaming. He leads game design projects and researches two main topics: on the one hand the potential of 3D visibility analysis, and on the other hand the complexity perspective on gaming and urban design. He is also the founder of Aisophyst, which provides consultancy based on 3D visibility analysis software.

Arthur van Bilsen, Ph.D.
Chair of Policy, Organization, Law & Gaming
Faculty of Technology, Policy and Management, Delft University of Technology
Jaffalaan 5, 2628 BX Delft, The Netherlands
Tel. +31 (0)15 2787239
Email: a.vanbilsen@tudelft.nl

REFERENCES

Aldrich, C. (2005), *Learning by Doing*. Pfeiffer-Wiley, San Francisco, CA.

Batty, M., Desyllas, J. and Duxbury, E. (2003), The discrete dynamics of small-scale spatial events: Agent-based models of mobility in carnivals and street parades. *International Journal of Geographical Information Science* 17, Issue. 7, pp. 673-697.

Bekebrede, G. and Mayer I.S. (2006), Build your seaport in a game and learn about complex systems. *Journal of Design Research* 5 (2): 273-298.

Benedikt, M.L. (1979), To take hold of space: isovist fields. *Environment and Planning B: Planning and Design* 6(1): 47-65.

Biederman, I. (1993), *Visual Object Recognition. Readings in Philosophy and Cognitive Science*. Editor A.I. Goldman. MIT Press, Cambridge, MA.

Cai, Y., Fan, Z., Wan, H., Gao, S., Lu, B. and Lim K.T. (2006), Hardware-accelerated collision detection for 3D virtual reality gaming. *Simulation & Gaming* 37(4), Sage.

Carvalho, R. and Batty M. (2003), *A rigorous definition of axial lines: ridges on isovist fields. Casa Working Paper Series (69).*

Csíkszentmihályi, M. (1990), *Flow: The Psychology of Optimal Experience*. Harper and Row, New York.

Darken, C.J. (2007), Computer Graphics-Based Models of Target Detection: Algorithms, Comparison to Human Performance, and Failure Modes. *The Journal of Defense Modeling and Simulation: Applications, Methodology, Technology* 4:390.

Duke, R.D. (2000), A personal perspective on the evolution of gaming. *Simulation & Gaming* 31(1): 79-85.

Duke, R.D. and Geurts J.L.A. (2004), *Policy Games for Strategic Management: Pathways into the Unknown*. Dutch University Press, Amsterdam.

Education Council (2003), *Leren in een kennissamenleving* [Dutch]. Verkenning, the Hague.

Egenfeldt-Nielsen, S. (2004), Practical barriers in using educational computer games. *On the Horizon* 12(1): 18-21.

Egenfeldt-Nielsen, S. (2005), *Beyond Edutainment – Exploring the Educational Potential of Computer Games*. PhD-thesis. University of Copenhagen, Copenhagen.

Epstein, R. and Kanwisher N. (1998), A cortical representation of the local visual environment. *Nature* 392: 598-601.

Fisher-Gewirtzmann, D. and Wagner I.A. (2003), Spatial openness as a practical metric for evaluating built-up environments. *Environment and Planning B: Planning and Design* 30.

Franz, G. and Wiener J.M. (2005), *Exploring isovist-based correlates of spatial behavior and experience*. Proceedings of the 5th Space Syntax Symposium, Delft, Techne Press.

Gee, J.P. (2003*) What video games have to teach us about learning and literacy*, Palgrave Macmillan.

Gibson, J.J. (1987), *The Ecological Approach to Visual Perception*, Lawrence Erlbaum Assoc.

Greenblat, C.S. (1975), Teaching with simulation games: a review of claims and evidence. In: C.S. Greenblat and R.D. Duke (eds.) *Gaming-Simulation: Rationale, Design And Applications*. John Wiley & Sons, New York: 270-284.

Greenblat, C.S. (1988), *Designing Games and Simulations: An Illustrated Handbook*. Sage Publications, Beverly Hills/London.

Greenblat, C.S. and Duke R.D. (1975), (eds.) *Gaming-Simulation: Rationale, Design And Applications*. John Wiley & Sons, New York.

Hillier, B. (1997), *The Hidden Geometry of Deformed Grids: or, why space syntax works when it looks as though it shouldn't*. Space Syntax First International Symposium, London.

Hillier, B. (1998), The Common Language of Space. *www.spacesyntax.org*.

Hillier, B. and Hanson J. (1984*), The Social Logic of Space*, Cambridge University Press, Cambridge.

Hoogendoorn, S.P. and Daamen W. (2007), *Microscopic calibration and validation of pedestrian models: cross-comparison of models using experimental data*. In: Schadschneider A., Pöschel T., Kühne R., Schreckenberg M. and Wolf D.E. (Eds.), Traffic and Granular Flow '05, Springer, Heidelberg, Berlin: 329-340.

Kaplan, R. and Kaplan S. (1989), *The Experience of Nature: A Psychological Perspective*. Cambridge University Press, Cambridge (UK).

Kriz, W.C. (2003), Creating Effective Learning Environments and Learning Organizations through Gaming Simulation Design. *Simulation and Gaming*, 34(4), 495–511.

Lynch, K. (1960), *The Image of the City*. MIT Press Cambridge, MA.

Marr, D. (1982), *Vision: A Computational Investigation into Human Representation and Processing of Visual Information*. W.H. Freeman, New York.

Mayer, I.S. and Mastik H. (2007), *Organizing and Learning through Gaming and Simulation*, Proceedings of ISAGA 2007, Eburon, Delft.

Mayer, I.S., Stegers-Jager, K. and Geertje B. (2007) *Spelend leren in virtuele werelden: Bouwstenen voor online gaming in het hoger onderwijs* [Dutch]. Wolters-Noordhoff, Groningen.

Mayer, I.S. and Veeneman W. (Eds.) (2002), Games in a World of Infrastructures. Simulation-games for Research, *Learning and Intervention*. Eburon, Delft.

Michael, D. and Chen S. (2006), *Serious games: Games that educate, train, and inform.* Thomson Course Technology Boston, MA.

Morello, E. and Ratti C. (2009), A digital image of the city: 3D isovists in Lynch's urban analysis. *Environment and Planning B: Planning and Design, advance online publication* 6 April 2009, doi:10.1068/b34144t.

Nes, A. van (2005), *Burglaries in the burglar's vicinity*. 5th Space Syntax Symposium, Delft, Techne Press, the Netherlands.

Newman, O. (1972), *Defensible Space: Crime Prevention through Urban Design*. New York, Macmillan.

Peponis J, Wineman J, Bafna S, Rashid M. and Kim S. H. (1998a), On the generation of linear representations of spatial configuration. *Environment and Planning B: Planning and Design* 25: 559-576.

Peponis J, Wineman J, Bafna S, Rashid M. and Kim S. H. (1998b), Describing plan configuration according to the covisibility of surfaces. *Environment and Planning B: Planning and Design* 25: 693-708.

Peponis J, Wineman J, Rashid M, Hong Kim S. and Bafna S. (1997), On the description of shape and spatial configuration inside buildings: convex partitions and their local properties. *Environment and Planning B: Planning and Design* 24:761-781.

Prensky, M. (2001) *Digital Game-Based Learning*. McGraw-Hill.

Prensky, M. (2007) How to teach with technology: Keeping both teachers and students comfortable in an era of exponential change. *Emerging Technologies for Learning* 2.

Salen, K. and Zimmerman E. (2004), *Rules of Play*. MIT Press, Cambridge, MA.

Sarradin, F. (2004), *Analyse morphologique des espaces ouverts urbains le long de parcours. École doctorale Mécanique, Thermique en Génie civil*. Nantes, Université de Nantes. Doctorat: 224.

Squire, K.D. (2004), *Replaying History: Learning world history through playing Civilization III*. PhD Thesis. Indiana University, Bloomington, IN.

Stamps, A.E.I. (2005), Visual permeability, locomotive permeability, and enclosure. *Environment and Behavior* 37(5): 587-619.

Teller, J. (2003), A spherical metric for the field-orientated analysis of complex urban open spaces. *Environment and Planning* B 30: 339-356.

Valve (2004), *HalfLife 2*. Bellevue, Washington, USA.

Van Bilsen, A. (2008), Mathematical Explorations in Urban and Regional Design. PhD Thesis, Delft University of Technology, Delft, The Netherlands. Available online: *www.aisophyst.nl.*

Van Bilsen, A. and Stolk E.H. (2008), *Solving Error Problems in Visibility Analysis for Urban Environments by Shifting From a Discrete to a Continuous Approach*. IEEE Proceedings, ICCSA 2008, June 30-July 3, Perugia, Italy.

Van Bilsen, A. (2009), *How can serious games benefit from 3D visibility analysis*, Proceedings of ISAGA 2009, June 29-July 3, Singapore.

Van Bilsen, A. and Stolk E.H. (2007), *The Potential of Isovist-Based Visibility Analysis. Architectural Annual*, 010 Publishers, Netherlands.

Van Bilsen, A., Bekebrede, G. and Mayer I.S. (2010), Understanding complex infrastructure systems by gaming. *Forthcoming*. Informatics in Education (April).

Van Bilsen, A. and R. Poelman (2009), 3D Visibility Analysis in Virtual Worlds: the Case of Supervisor. *Forthcoming*. Accepted for CONVR2009, November 5-6, Sydney, Australia.

Van Eck, R. (2006), Digital game-based learning: It's not just the digital natives who are restless. *EDUCAUSE review*, March/April, 16-30.

Yarbus, A.L. (1967), *Eye movements and vision*. Plenum Press, New York.

In: Interactive and Digital Media for Education in Virtual … ISBN: 978-1-61668-844-8
Editor: Cai Yiyu

Chapter 7

MEDIATED AND ENGAGED LEARNING USING COTS VIDEO GAMES IN ASD SPECIAL EDUCATION

Norman Kiak Nam Kee and Noel Kok Hwee Chia
Nanyang Technical University, Singapore

ABSTRACT

People with autism spectrum disorders (ASD) have impairments in communication, social interaction and imagination but not in their understanding of physical causality. Potentially, people with ASD can learn and win games where causality is within the design, such as racing, shooting, puzzle and comic fighting games. Instant feedbacks have helped to develop their eye-hand coordination, visual selective attention, memory, and executive control. However, human mediation of symbolic learning is still needed to help a child with ASD to construct the understanding of the game symbols (signifiers) for their associated meaning (signified) in game semiotic domains.

The educational use of Commercial-Off-The-Shelf (COTS) video games in special education is a relatively unexplored research territory, with no formal endorsement for learning by children with ASD. This chapter focuses on mediated and engaged learning in special education for children with ASD using COTS video games. Feuerstein's Dynamic Assessment and Mediated Learning Experience (MLE) are applied to mediate the learning from video games for social-cultural learning. The mediated learning proposed here aims to first transform the knowledge into action and then action into knowledge through human mediation of transcendence of application and generalization.

Keywords: autism; special education; mediated learning; engaged learning; COTS video games

Introduction

Autism Spectrum Disorder

Autism or autism spectrum disorders (ASD) collectively as a syndrome affects 60 per 10,000 people (Scahill & Bears, 2009) with about 50 per cent not mentally impaired (Poon, 2009; Carpenter et al., 2009). Recently, much media attention has been drawn on the alarming increase in diagnosed cases worldwide of ASD people (Poon, 2009; Carpenter et al., 2009; Lawrence & Karen, 2009). To date, Chia (2008) has reviewed existing definitions of ASD and proposed the following definition:

> "A neurodevelopmental syndrome of constitutional origin (i.e., genetic and epigenetic causes), whose onset is usually around first three years of birth, with empathizing or mentalizing deficits that result in a triad of impairments in communication, social interaction and imagination, but may, on the other hand, displays (especially by autistic savants) or hides (especially by autistic crypto-savants) a strong systemizing drive that accounts for a distinct triad of strengths in good attention to detail, deep narrow interests, and islets of ability (p.10)."

However, people with ASD do not have impairment in their understanding of physical causality, and might even be superior relative to mental-age matched controls (Baron-Cohen et al., 1986; Wakabayashi et al., 2007). This intact systematizing ability (Wakabayashi et al., 2007; Lawson et al., 2004) is defined as the drive to analyze and build systems, with the aim of understanding and predicting non-agentive events. Lawson et al. (2004) elaborate:

> "Systems can be technical (e.g., the workings of a machine), natural (e.g., the process of coastal erosion), abstract (e.g., mathematics), motoric (e.g., a guitar playing technique), taxonomic (e.g., a criterion for ordering compact discs) or social (e.g., a taxation system). When confronted with systems such as these we don't analyze them in terms of emotions or mental states. Rather, we examine relationships between components and correlations between events which then allow us to understand any underlying rules that may be relevant. By identifying regularities between the input, operations, and output of a system it becomes possible to predict the behavior of a system" (p.302).

Video Games and Special Education

Video games are essentially computer programs designed and built based on logic, running on highly customized and purpose built computer systems or game consoles for game playing. The human computer interfaces for interaction have evolved over time and the latest Nintendo Wii interfaces provide a 3-D input for working with 3-D virtual worlds (Sreedharan et al., 2007). Video game playing is an activity loved by most children and adults, with or without special needs (Lipschultz, 2009; Mayo, 2009; Jolley, 2008; Gee, 2007a, 2007b; Shaffer, 2006; Simpson, 2005; Kirriemuir & McFarlane, 2004; Houghton et al., 2004). Prensky (2006) has even coined the term "Digital Native" for their natural inclination and ability to appreciate and learn from digital technology. He is a strong advocate for digital game-based learning (Prensky, 2007) and has even proposed new roles for trainers and teachers to leverage on it for the 21st century relevance and success (Prensky, 2006). Some studies tried using videos with VLE and some facilitation for teaching social skills in a café (Mitchell et al., 2007; Parsons et al., 2004), while another used an avatar from a custom built software program to facilitate learning of four emotions (Moore et al., 2005). The authors of this chapter believe the complexity and unpredictability of human behavior requires intensive human mediation.

Video games are a form of interactive digital media (IDM). Most studies (e.g., Cromby et al., 1996; Ira, 1997; Brown et al., 1998; Reid & Campbell, 2006; Lahav & Mioduser, 2004; Clancy et al., 2006; Grynszpan et al., 2008) involving the use of IDM for special education includes development of custom built software applications from research grants. Expensive and sensitive hardware is also used during development, limiting its availability and reach to all children with special needs for education. Being a parent of three adolescent sons with ASD, the first author of this chapter works as a full-time lecturer in special needs education with a main focus on autism in collaborative partnership with the second author in the same field. This chapter proposes to use relatively affordable COTS video games in dedicated game console players for ASD special education.

People with ASD may need dedicated game consoles for game playing instead of video games running on desktop personal computers (PC). Children with ASD may suddenly switch off the PC power when frustrated in game play. This often results in corrupted operating systems, requiring reinstallation of operating systems. Moreover, personal computers running on Windows require frequent patching of the operating system. Sometimes, new updated drivers are also needed after patching with reconfiguration for game purposes. Dedicated game consoles are certainly positive in that they are able to recover from erratic behaviors of sudden switching off of power and unconventional use of game controllers. The first author began his research interest in COTS video games when he observed his two ASD children playing and achieving some level of success with Nintendo DS and Nintendo Wii games, without using the game manuals. Nintendo DS or Nintendo Wii game playing consoles are affordable, widely available and reliable, even with rough use and popular (Moreno-Ger et al., 2009). Moreover, a proven world-wide commercial entity, such as Nintendo Company, is able to continually fund research and development for continuity and sustainability of the platform.

People normally need to refer to game manuals before their play. However, children's interest and perseverance in games of their interest have led them to intuitively not only discover the properties, rules and procedures that must be mastered in order to become a "player" (Rosas et al., 2003) but also to win the games. Perhaps learning is more through situated cognition (Wilson & Myres, 2000) of the complex environment of the games. Currently, behavioral and cognitive-behavioral interventions are endorsed and supported in special education (Martin & Christopher, 2008) for ASD people education. Shafer (2006) in his book "*How computer games help children learn*" revealed that good computer or video games allow "children to live in worlds that they are curious about, or afraid of, or want desperately to try out" (p. 24) and implicitly it is because they want to understand the rules, roles and consequences of those worlds. Squire at the University of Wisconsin-Madison and director of the Games, Learning, and Society Program has reported that video game-based learning is an emerging paradigm for instruction (Squire, 2008).

A literature search using online databases (conducted on 8 August 2009), from peer-reviewed journals (see Table 1), revealed that research on the educational use of the COTS video games in special education, is relatively unexplored compared to mainstream education.

Jonassen et al. (2008) have crystallized the essential attributes for meaningful learning to be active, constructive, intentional, authentic, and cooperative learning. Kee (2009a, 2009b) has found the attributes to apply for autistic people learning, where they construct their learning (Lainema, 2009) in game play. Jonassen et al. have also highlighted some of Gee's (2007a, pp. 221-227) thirty-six learning principles used in well designed modern game design (Gee, 2007a, pp. 221-227) of successful COTS video games. Other studies (see Wilson et al., 2009) considered other key gaming features to be necessary for learning which includes fantasy, rules/goals, sensory stimuli, challenge, mystery, and control but were not clear as to whether one attribute had a greater impact on learning than another, or whether it was the combination of attributes that led to success.

Table 1. Results of online database search

Subject	Education	Special education	Video games	Autism	Education & Video games	Special education & video games	Autism & video games
ERIC & PsycINFO (hits)	1,009,695 (100%)	51,928 (5.14%)	1,080 (0.10%)	18,973 (1.88%)	223 (0.02%)	7 (0.00%)	1 (0.00%)
Proquest (hits)	1,056,420 (100%)	67,579 (6.40%)	155,415 (14.71%)	19,471 (1.84%)	1350 (0.13%)	19 (0.00%)	21 (0.00%)

Subjectivities Statement and Research Objectives

The objectivity as researchers is situated within subjective thoughts influenced by personal histories, cultural worldviews and professional experiences (Lewis-Beck et al., 2004). The authors of this chapter would like to explicate these influences. Being aware of how their subjectivity may shape their own research inquiry and its outcomes (Peshkin, 1988), the authors of this chapter desire to collect trustworthy data in this study. Their collective view is that all ASD individuals are unique and may learn or appreciate the same learning situation differently due to their sensory, cognitive, and perceptual differences, though they may have some common autistic traits. The authors believe this also happens to neurotypical (mainstream) adults. For example, many batches of trainee teachers in authors' classes have watched the same video but revealed differing constructions of their perceptions and understanding for the same learning event when they shared through class discussions or through their written reflections. The authors have noticed that the subjects construct their own knowledge by exploration and observation of others than by didactic means. Implicitly, the theoretical perspective adopted in this chapter is social constructionism (Crotty, 1998, pp. 52-57) that is transactional and subjective (Guba & Lincoln, 2005). Game players thus interact with the game environment and game avatars and make sense using situated cognition (Jonassen & Land, 2000) with learning and building of their identity in the process

(Shaffer, 2006; Gee, 2007a). The "social" in social constructionism need not involve persons (and therefore need not be 'social' in that sense)(Crotty, 1998. p. 55), but rather with computer artifacts that interact and transact with the player of the game. Interaction of the ASD children with the objects and environment created by the simulated world is thus also social. The authors' ontology is relativism (Guba & Lincoln, 2005, p. 193) that is realities perceived by the game players are local and specific constructions and co-constructed realities (with mediators). It is assumed that these transactional interactions will lead to learning. In this chapter, the authors shall therefore use the narrative-type narrative inquiry (Polkinghorne, 1995) to explicate their understanding of the pedagogy and learning of the three subjects of this study retrospectively. Crotty (1988, p. 60) has identified the work of Karl Mannheim (1893-1947) and from Berger and Luckmann's "The Social Construction of Reality" (1967) to be the key scholars in social constructionism. The authors have found the works of James Paul Gee (Gee, 2007a, 2007b), Marc Prensky (2001, 2006) and David Williamson Shaffer (2006), key to understanding what video games have to teach or help children learn.

This chapter focuses on engaged and fun learning in special education for children with ASD using COTS video games. Feuerstein's Dynamic Assessment and Mediated Learning Experience (MLE) are applied to mediate the learning from video games for social-cultural learning. The mediated learning proposed here aims to first transform the knowledge into action and then action into knowledge through human mediation of transcendence of application and generalization. The authors would argue that people with ASD have an intact systematizing ability that should enable them to perceive the underlying rules for playing and winning the game, which are explicated through predictable cause and effect logic, especially in games where immediate feedback provides means to associate meaning with game moves (e.g. puzzles, shooting, racing, and comic fighting).

MEDIATED LEARNING USING COTS VIDEO GAME

Why Mediated Learning?

People learn meanings of practically all their words by association of "*hearing those noises as they accompany actual situations in life*" (Hayakawa & Hayakawa, 1990, p. 36). These meanings are constructed through multiple sociocultural interactions of parents, teachers, peers and the community in defining the type of leaning interaction occurring between subjects and their environment (Kozulin, 2002). People with ASD have impairments in communication and social interaction and will therefore lack the sociocultural interactions needed to construct meanings derived from social transactions. Even neurotypical adults from the different institutional setting of legal practice will encounter hermeneutical impasse (Moortz, 2007, p. 145) of legal meanings without enculturation into the new setting. "*Symbols used in society and their symbolized meanings have no necessary connection and are independent of each other*" (Hayakawa & Hayakawa, 1990, pp.16-17). Human mediators are therefore needed to mediate the meaning (signified) of the symbols (signifier) used in society (semiotic domains) (Gee, 2007a). Jonassen and Land (2000), asserts:

> "when we investigate learning phenomena, we are obligated to consider not only the performance of the learners, but also the sociocultural and sociohistorical setting in which the performance occurs and tools and mediation systems that learners use to make meaning" (p. vi)

The search for ways to mediate the learning of semiotic domains lead the authors to Feuerstein's theory of dynamic assessment of structural cognitive modifiability (SCM) (Feuerstein et al., 2002; Feuerstein, 2000) and mediated learning experience (MLE) (Feuerstein et al., 1999; Mentis et al., 2008; Seng et al., 2003), where cultural deprivation has its effects on cognitive development and intellectual performance requiring MLE for learning. People with ASD generally do suffer from cultural deprivation as they lack a natural ability to socially interact with others in society and have thus become alienated from their own culture (Feuerstein et al., 2002, p. 49). Parents will have difficulty helping their ASD children construct the social practice, cultural field and habitus (Webb et al., 2002), terms used by Bourdieu. Feuerstein's theories have proposed the triple ontogeny of human development, comprised of biological, cultural and mediated learning experience (Feuerstein, Feuerstein, et al., 2006). This stems from the belief in brain plasticity (Lebeer, 2008; Tan & Seng, 2008; Feuerstein, Rand, et al., 2006) and learning possible across the lifespan (Shing et al., 2008) where intensive social and cognitive interventions are involved to mediate learning. Professor Reuven Feuerstein has worked with a large number of children who manifested massive intellectual and academic dysfunctioning and are culturally deprived for emigration to Israel. He developed the theory of mediated learning experience (MLE) over the period of 1950-1963 based on his belief and operationalization of SCM (Feuerstein et al., 1999) to make a positive difference and contribution to mankind. Grigorenko (2009) from Yale University has compared and contrasted the main features of dynamic testing and assessment (DT/A), where MLE (1963) is an approach, with response to intervention (RTI), a relatively newer approach (1982), supported by Individual with Disabilities Education Improvement Act (IDIEA; 2004). She found that they belong to the same family of methodologies in psychology and education whose key feature is in blending assessment and intervention in one holistic activity. "Because DT/A has been around much longer than RTI, it makes sense to consider the accomplishments and frustrations accumulated in the field of DT/A" (Grigorenko, 2009, p. 111)

Feuerstein et al (1999) defined MLE

> "as a quality of interaction between the organism and its environment. This quality is ensured by the interposition of an initiated, intentional human being who mediates the stimuli impinging on the organism. This mode of interacting is parallel to and qualitatively different from the more generalized and more pervasive modality of interaction between world and organism referred to as "direct exposure to stimuli" (p.7)

The role played by the human mediator in MLE is in the development of autoplasticity and flexibility of the efficient learner (Feuerstein et al., 1999). The twelve types of quality MLE interaction as in Figure 1, of which the three core and essential qualities are mediation of intentionality and reciprocity, mediation of meaning, and mediation of transcendence. The metaphor of an organism Amoeba was chosen as the processes by which amoeba moves and ingest its food is by means of dynamic and adaptive processes in the lived in environment.

What to Mediate?

What to mediate depends on the educational opportunities available to mediate learning in video games that people with ASD choose to play. What to mediate is tightly coupled with how to mediate. Perhaps, the question is what video games can be used for people with ASD to mediate learning. The first author of this chapter will share from his findings (Kee, 2009a, 2009b) on the insights gained from observing his own children.

Perhaps, the first critical consideration is to use only those video game titles that children with ASD have already expressed interest in. The first author discovered that his sons do check out the Nintendo or YouTube websites for videos of new games, and have thereafter made some choices. The second teenage subject has high functioning ASD and sensory integration issues where he likes to cup his ears when he senses uncomfortable sounds from the environment. He has limited verbal expressive ability and is currently attending a special education school. He knows how to use the computer for Internet surfing for topics of his interest, such as lifts, Luigi (his favorite Nintendo character) and trains, using Google search. He discovers pictures, videos and even toys on the Internet and would point out on the computer screen, objects or video games of his interest. His monitor screen is full of pictures he downloads from the web with many new folder shortcuts filling up the desktop screen. “There is a strong link between motivation and self-determination. Most parents of autistic children are well aware of this” (Siegal, 2003, p.239). The first author witnessed his demonstration of curiosity, exploration, perseverance and imitation of visual hints of the video game affordances, leading to winning some levels of the game when the video games are of his choice and interest.

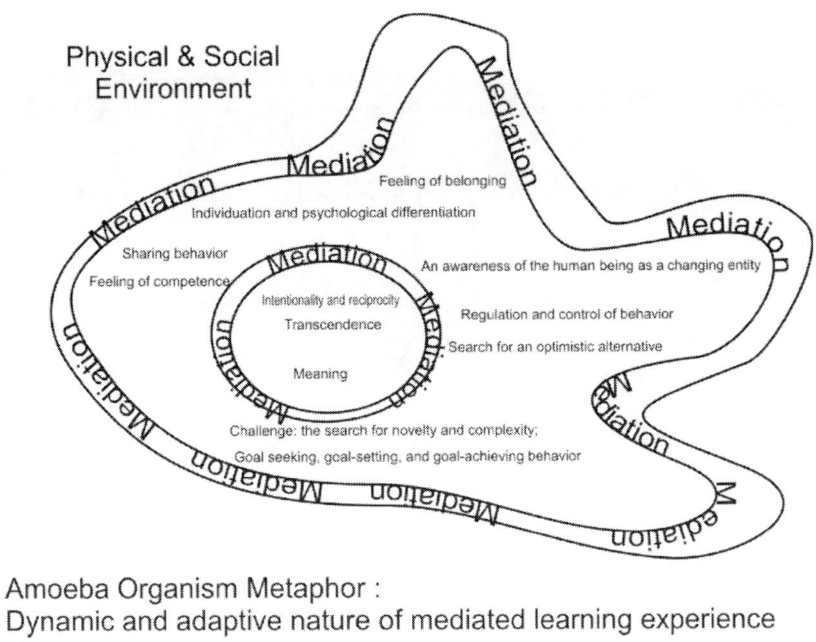

Figure 1. 12 criteria of mediation.

For example, he completed a 3x3 configuration 3-D puzzle in “Mario Super Sluggers” game in five minutes (see Figure 2). This task is not easy, as every one of the nine pieces can be rotated in four directions with nine possible positions. He probably learns by keen observation and reflection of his visual manipulations. While travelling on the public transports, we observed that neurotypical adolescent people, as well as the studied adolescent subjects with ASD, like to play action games. People with ASD should be able to learn to play video games by themselves when the games involve causality with immediate feedback. The instant feedbacks develop their eye-hand coordination (Gee, 2007a), visual selective attention (Green & Bavelier, 2003), memory, and executive control (Boot et al., 2008). They are able to do so as they have no impairments in their understanding of physical causality, and may even be superior relative to mental-age matched controls (Baron-Cohen, et al., 1986). However, the video game needs to capture their interest and motivate them to explore the game. Continuity in game play depends on the perception of fun and opportunity to learn from failures while having fun. Generally, computer-based learning games developed by educators do not allow the freedom to veer far away from the learning goals to have fun. Nintendo games intentionally design their games to allow this behavior. For example, in Nintendo 'Paper Mario', players can choose not to save the world even after repeated request not to give it up. In Nintendo "Super Mario 64", players can go back to games after they have won and play it again with or without further incentives. The first author observed that his children sometimes enjoy certain courses within the games and would like to experience it again. Perhaps, it is therapeutic and provides some form of desired sensory modulation. The intentional provisions for such behavior possibly satisfy their curiosity and tendency for unorthodox moves, thereby encouraging emotional acceptance of games.

An important note is that we have filtered out those video games that we have considered as undesirable such as those with violence (scenes of blood and gore), sexual or criminal themes, which incorporates the General Aggression Model (Anderson et al., 2007) in game play (Barlett et al., 2009).

Start Complete

Figure 2. Puzzle activity at start and completion (5 minutes).

Among three subjects, the eldest is high functioning and included in mainstream schools. He started playing video games when he was four years old. His first game console was Nintendo 64, where he played "Mario Kart", a racing car game involving Nintendo iconic characters such as Mario, Luigi, Donkey Kong, Peach and others. The game rich color graphics, sound effects, lively and cheerful music, realistic animations and cheerful looking comic characters to play with, attracted him to try the game. He was initially showed how to play "correctly" by pressing the appropriate buttons to move forward. By choice, he went backwards and tried exploring around. He was happy and pleased with the new "playground". Though his action was perplexing, he was allowed to continue playing the way he wanted. The game was only setup on weekends. It was surprising to hear celebration music of his winning a trophy for competing and winning races after some weeks. The existence of trophies for winning a set of four circuit races was not known as the authors did not play the game. On hindsight, it appears that fun and engaging elements in game play are absolutely essential to interest a child to play. The first author remembered trying various educational computer software titles considered "good", leveraging on his knowledge and expertise in computer based learning education, while working as a project leader in the Curriculum and Development Institute of Singapore, Ministry of Education, but to no avail to interest him. Looking back, patience was critical as it allowed him time and freedom to learn from failures (Shank, 2002). His exploration of what's interesting with active manipulation, observation and reflection of the cause and effects relationship, as well as just in time, simple and direct visual instructions superimposed in game play (see Figure 3) probably help to sustain his continued interest to overcome challenges in game. The authors believe the rich multimedia environment is authentic to him and engages him to intentionally learn how to play and win the games. Games involving causality constructs, such as racing, shooting, puzzles, comic fighting, exploration for treasures and manipulation skills involving equipments, tools, martial arts, sports and others, are eventually mastered by him. Another salient observation is the importance of winning. They will look for cheat codes or ways to cheat if possible. For example, they may terminate the game halfway if they are not going to win, apply cheat codes searched from the web or even observe each other for techniques to overcome challenges. The second son of the first author has even drowned the Nintendo DS in water when he could not overcome the challenges in "Tetris" game. The first author learnt this truth only after the embarrassing report from Nintendo Japan revealing the faulty set was drowned in water. Insistence and firmness thereafter was made for all to play in a fixed location, well away from the toilet, with rules and logical consequences on appropriate game play.

Just in time visually explicit help Cinematic authentic game play

Figure 3. Just in time help and cinematic authentic game play.

The youngest among three subjects is high functioning and verbal but also has emotional behavior disorder. Thus, his invisible disability requires special education settings to maximize his potential. He likes to play “Animal Crossing: City Folk” and is immersed in the virtual world. He has fun pushing snow balls, fishing, catching insects, buying toys he likes for his home, donating his collection of fossils to the museum and even enjoying a cup of coffee in a café, where a beagle dog will sing his favorite songs on Saturdays. Simulations of the four seasons of the year, opening hours of Tom Nook’s shop and seasonal fishes are embedded in game play scenarios. His learning experiences were mediated while in game play. The game provided the context, complexity, continuity of interaction for him to construct understanding of symbols used in the virtual world. He was helped to appreciate societal functions and responsibilities, such as the need to work for “bells” to pay up his house mortgage (see Figure 4). Other concepts, such as deferred gratification, are gradually introduced, to help him construct the understanding of need for savings in the Nintendo bank to build up the ability to purchase expensive items when desired. This is a mediation involving knowledge-into-action (Crookall & Thorngate, 2009) where a deferred gratification concept is explicated by his actions of saving and subsequently gratification, when he purchases what he likes. He even enjoys the feeling of success (evidenced by a smile on his face and boasting to his parent) when he donates “bells” for societal improvement projects, as he witnesses claps and acknowledgement from other game avatars while doing so.

Fun: Make big snow ball & fishing

Buying house

Selling goods for bells

Payment of house mortgage

Figure 4. Fun and Paying Mortgage of House.

How to Mediate?

Essentially, by active observations and through trial and error, the authors of this chapter use simple conversations of symbols or words that their subjects can understand to help them make sense of the VLE, such as "Animal Crossing: City Folks". The learning potential and progress of the subjects is determined more by trial and error attempts of mediation of intentionality/reciprocity, mediation of meaning and mediation of transcendence while their subjects are in game play. For example, by analogy of daddy needing to work to earn money to pay the house mortgage to one subject's game play of fishing to earn bells to pay the mortgage, mediation for transcendence was attempted. This facilitates action-into-knowledge (Crookall & Thorngate, 2009), that is, the subject's actions of fishing, harvesting fruits are equivalent to the knowledge of working on a job in society. Mediation of competence was done by describing to the subject how well he is doing by his wealth in bells and his rich collection of toys and expensive furnishings in his home. The continual social interactions with avatars (e.g. conversational transactions, business transactions) and social processes with other game artifacts (e.g. fishing, harvesting fruits, picking up sea shells to exchange for bells) allows the construction of knowledge with understanding of societal symbols and their meanings resulting in situated experiential learning (Wideman et al., 2007).

Below is an example of how mediation may be carried out:

Step 1

1. Select Video Game (e.g. Animal Crossing on Wii)
2. Observe a subject in game play (e.g. shown intense interest to harvest pears, coconuts or fishing to sell to Tom Nook for bells and buy some of his shop's goodies)
3. Deliberate on opportunities to mediate learning or zone of proximal development (ZPD). (e.g. ability to repeat activities of collecting fruits, sell fruits and thereafter purchasing goods of his interest, suggesting readiness to construct the concept of work in society)
4. Plan lesson dynamically focusing on process of learning.

Step 2: Mediation of Intentionality and Reciprocity (example)

1. Dynamically assess the subject's readiness to engage in conversation about his activities.
2. If ready, praise the subject that he is making a lot of bells and becoming rich enough to buy a lot of goodies. Check for his response.
3. If the subject responds positively to selection and framing of the activity to focus, move on to the mediation of meaning.

Step 3: Mediation of Meaning

Goal: Dynamically encourage the subject to use words like work, job, earnings, salary in his activity so as to allow multiple opportunity to associate words with activity for construction of meaning in doing.

1. If the subject reciprocates positively, attempt mediation of symbols used in society for the activities (e.g. I see you are working very hard, collecting fruits to sell to Tom Nook for bells. Daddy is also working, teaching and writing papers in NTU to earn money).
2. Use more examples, so that the subject becomes familiar with words, commonly used to describe the activity. Eventually, check to see if the subject could independently use the introduced words in context of activity.

Step 4: Mediation of Transcedence

Goal: Promote the generalization to settings beyond the game activity

Possible Strategy: Use of analogy through token economy of information in Tables 2-5 below.

Table 2.

Virtual World (bells currency)				Home World (stars currency)			
Job	Activity	Goods/ Service	Unit Price	Job	Activity	Goods/ Service	Unit Price
Farmer	Harvest	Pears	100	Laundry-man	Wash clothes with washing machine	Clean set of clothes	5
Farmer	Harvest	Coconut	500	Laundry-man	Iron clothes	Ironed set of clothes	10
Fisher-man	Fishing	Type A	300	Cleaner	Sweep floor	Cleaned floor	5
Fisher-man	Fishing	Type B	1500	Cleaner	Mop floor	Mopped floor	10

Table 3.

Virtual World (Tom Nook's Shop)		Home World (Home Shop)	
Item	Unit Price (bells)	Item	Unit Price (stars)
T.V. Set	3000	Hamburger sweet	5
Washing Machine	2000	Kit Kat	20
House Mortgage	200000	Nintendo DS	10000

Table 4.

Food Court (Tiong Bahru Kopi Tiam)				Food Court (Tiong Bahru Kopi Tiam) - Extension			
Job	Activity	Goods/ Service	Unit Price ($)	Job	Activity	Goods/ Service	Salary ($)
Chicken rice stall owner	Selling	Chicken rice	3.50	Chicken rice stall owner	Selling	Chicken rice	3500
Drink stall owner	Selling	Coke	1.50	Drink stall owner	Selling	Coke	3000

Table 5. Possible Extensions of Learning

Concepts	Examples
Profit – Loss Opportunity Cost	Development of strategic thinking (example : Growing more coconut trees instead of pear trees as each harvested coconut fetches more bells.)
Addition Multiplication	How many coconuts do I need to sell to buy the grandfather clock at 3000 bells?
Productivity Entrepreneurship	Development of altruism (Example : Donating fossils found to the museum for the benefit of all in the town to preview)

CONCLUSION

The educational use of COTS video games in special education should be seriously considered for formal use as it is a medium that not only interests neurotypical people but also people with special needs. People with ASD can learn from video games where causality is in the design with the provision of immediate feedback. Moreover, COTS video games can potentially provide a consistent, continuous social context for ASD people to socially construct an understanding of complex societal concepts. The authors propose the use of Feuerstein's Dynamic Assessement and Mediated Learning Experience (MLE) to mediate the learning from video games for sociocultural learning with the final goal of transforming the knowledge-into-action (Kriz, 2009) and then action-into-knowledge (Crookall & Thorngate, 2009) through human mediation of transcendence of application and generalization. Rogoff (1990, 1993), a developmental psychologist has also advocated apprenticeship (cultural), guided participation (interpersonal) and appropriation (personal), where humans do mediate for the sociocultural activity of learning.

AUTHOR INFO

Norman Kiak Nam KEE M.Tech, M.Ed, B.Sc, Dip.Ed. Tech, Dip.Ed, a former secondary school teacher, is a lecturer with the Early Childhood and Special Needs Education Academic Group at the National Institute of Education, Nanyang Technological University, Singapore. Prior to this current appointment, he was a specialist writer/project leader with the Curriculum Development Institute of Singapore (CDIS), Ministry of Education, to develop the *Dynamic Mathematics Series* – a computer-based learning software - whose *Jungle Survival with Quadratic Equations* (a CD-ROM) has won three international awards in 1997: the Macromedia People's Choice Award for Educational Multimedia in San Francisco, USA; the International Digital Media Award for Best Educational CD-ROM Overall in Toronto, Canada; and the International Digital Media Award for Best Educational CD-ROM in K-12 Category in Toronto, Canada. Later, he left the CDIS to join Singapore Polytechnic to set up and maintain its e-learning infra-structure. A former Ministry of Education scholar (1993) at the SEAMEO Regional Education Centre for Science and Mathematics (RECSAM), Penang, Malaysia, Mr Kee was an evaluation panel committee member at the National Infocomm Competency Centre (NICC), Singapore, from 2003-2006, contributing to the development of professional certification in IT education. Currently, he is pursuing his PhD research study on autism spectrum disorders at the National Institute of Education.

Noel Kok Hwee CHIA Ed.D, M.Ed, B.Ed.St, B.Ed, PGDES, FCP, FCoT, a former teacher in the Gifted Education Programme, is an Assistant Professor with the Early Childhood and Special Needs Education Academic Group at the National Institute of Education, Nanyang Technological University, Singapore. A former reading specialist with the School Psychological Service, Ministry of Education, Singapore, he is the only board certified educational therapist registered with the American Association of Educational Therapists outside the United States as well as a board certified diplomate (Special Education) with the American Academy of Special Education Professionals. He is also a registered professional counsellor with the Australian Institute of Professional Counsellors. He sits on the Educational Standards Collaborative Committee of the International Standards Collaborative Committee of the International Association of Counselors and Therapists based in Pennsylvania, USA. In Singapore, he sits as a member on the Ministry of Community Development, Youth and Sports (MCYS) Advisory Board/Discharge Committee. Currently, he is a Lee Kong Chian Research Fellow researching on Singapore Children's Literature in English (1965-2005) at the Lee Kong Chian Reference Library, National Library Board, Singapore.

REFERENCES

Anderson, C. A., Gentile, D. A., & Buckley, K. E. (2007). *Violent video game effects on children and adolescents : theory, research, and public policy*. New York: Oxford University Press.

Barlett, C. P., Anderson, C. A. & Swing, E. L. (2009). Video Game Effects Confirmed, Suspected, and Speculative: A Review of the Evidence. *Simulation and Gaming*, *40*(3), 377-403. doi:10.1177/1046878108327539

Baron-Cohen, S., Frith, U., & Leslie, A. M. (1986). Mechanical, behavioural and intentional understanding of picture stories in autistic children. *British Journal of Developmental Psychology*, *4*(2), 113-125.

Boot, W. R., Kramer, A. F., Simons, D. J., Fabiani, M., & Gratton, G. (2008). The effects of video game playing on attention, memory, and executive control. Acta Psychologica, 129(3), 387-398.

Brown, D. J., Standen, P. J., Cobb, S. V., Riva, G., Wiederhold, B. K., & Molinari, E. (1998). Virtual environments special needs and evaluative methods. In *Virtual environments in clinical psychology and neuroscience: Methods and techniques in advanced patient-therapist interaction.* (pp. 91-102). Amsterdam, The Netherlands: IOS Press.

Carpenter, L. A., Soorya, L., & Halpern, D. (2009). Asperger's syndrome and high-functioning autism. *Pediatric Annals*, *38*(1), 30-35.

Chia, N.K.H. (2008). Autistic savant: A need to re-define autism spectrum disorder(ASD). *Special Educational Needs Monograph Series*. Singapore: Cobee Publishing House.

Clancy, T. A., Rucklidge, J. J., & Owen, D. (2006). Road-Crossing Safety in Virtual Reality: A Comparison of Adolescents With and Without ADHD. *Journal of Clinical Child & Adolescent Psychology, 35*(2), 203-215.

Crookall, D., & Thorngate, W. (2009). Acting, Knowing, Learning, Simulating, Gaming. *Simulation and Gaming, 40*(1), 8-26. doi:10.1177/1046878108330364

Cromby, J. J., Standen, P. J., & Brown, D. J. (1996). The potentials of virtual environments in the education and training of people with learning disabilities. *Journal of Intellectual Disability Research, 40*(6), 489-501.

Crotty, M. (1998). *The foundations of social research*. London: Sage Publications.

Feuerstein, R., Klein, P. S. & Tannenbaum, A. J. (1999). *Mediated Learning Experience (MLE): Theoretical, Psychosocial and Learning Principles*. London, UK : Freund Publishing House.

Feuerstein, R.S. (2000). Dynamic cognitive assessment and the instrumental enrichment program: Origins and development. In Kozulin, A., & Rand, Y. (Eds.), *Experience of mediated learning : an impact of Feuerstein's theory in education and psychology*. Amsterdam, The Netherlands: Pergamon Press.

Feuerstein, R., Feuerstein, R. S., Falik, L., & Rand, Y. (2002). *The Dynamic Assessment of Cognitive Modifiability (2nd Ed.)*. Tel Aviv, Israel: ICELP Publications.

Feuerstein, R., Feuerstein, R. S., Falik, L., & Rand, Y. (2006). *Creating and Enhancing Cognitive Modifiability: The Feuerstein Instrumental Enrichment Program*. Tel Aviv, Israel: ICELP Publications.

Feuerstein, R., Rand, Y. & Feuerstein, R. S. (2006). *Don't accept me as I am : helping the Low Functioning Person Excel(Rev. and Enlarged Ed.*) Tel Aviv, Israel: ICELP Publications.

Gee, J. P. (2007a). *What video games have to teach us about learning and literacy*. New York, NY: Palgrave Macmillan

Gee, J. P. (2007b). *Good video games + good learning: Collected essays on video games, learning and literacy*. New York, NY: Peter Lang

Grigorenko, E. L. (2009). Dynamic Assessment and Response to Intervention: Two Sides of One Coin. *Journal of Learning Disabilities, 42*(2), 111-132.

Green, C. S., & Bavelier, D. (2003). Action video game modifies visual selective attention. *Nature, 423*(6939), 534-537.

Grynszpan, O., Martin, J.-C., & Nadel, J. (2008). Multimedia interfaces for users with high functioning autism: An empirical investigation. *International Journal of Human-Computer Studies, 66*(8), 628-639.

Guba, E. G. & Lincoln, Y. S. (2005). Paradigmatic controversies, contradictions, and emerging confluences. In *The Sage Handbook of Qualitative Research*(3rd ed., pp. 191-215). London, UK: Sage Publications Ltd.

Hayakawa, S. I. & Hayakawa, A. R. (1990). *Language in thought and action* (5th ed.). Orlando, FL: Harcourt, Inc.

Houghton, S., Milner, N., West, J., Douglas, G., Lawrence, V., Whiting, K., et al. (2004). Motor control and sequencing of boys with Attention-Deficit/Hyperactivity Disorder (ADHD) during computer game play. *British Journal of Educational Technology, 35*(1), 21-34.

Ira, V. B. (1997). Virtual reality & mobility skills. *The Exceptional Parent, 27*(11), 50.

Jolley, K. (2008). Video Games to Reading: Reaching out to Reluctant Readers. *English Journal, 97*(4), 81-86.

Jonassen, D. H. & Land, S. M. (2000). *Theoretical Foundations of Learning Environments*. Boston, MA: Lawrence Erlbaum Associates.

Jonassen, D., Howland, J., Marra, J. & Crismond (2008). *Meaningful Learning with Technology (3rd ed.)*. NJ: Allyn & Bacon

Kee K. N. (2009a). Harnessing Commercial Off The Shelf (COTS) Video Games in Special Education: A Retrospective Reflection of Pedagogy and Learning observed with three Autistic Children in Game Play. In Kee K. N. (Ed.) *"Learn to Game, Game to Learn" International Simulation And Gaming Association 40th Annual Conference 29 June to 3 July 2009, Singapore* (pp. 1-8). Singapore: The International Simulation and Gaming Association.

Kee K. N. (2009b). Informal learning from video games of three autistic children in a family: A case study. *The Journal of READING & LITERACY, 1*(1), 45-60. Retrieved October 1, 2009, from *http://www.srl.org.sg/www/downloads/JRL_Vol1_No1_2009.pdf*

Kirriemuir, J., & McFarlane, A. (2004). Literature review in games and learning. *Futurelab*, 7. Retrieved July 30, 2009, from *http://www.futurelab.org.uk/resources/documents/lit_reviews/Games_Review.pdf*

Kozulin, A. (2002). Sociocultural Theory and the Mediated Learning Experience. *School Psychology International, 23*(1), 7-35.

Kriz, W. C. (2009). Bridging the Gap: Transforming Knowledge Into Action Through Gaming and Simulation. *Simulation Gaming, 40*(1), 28-29.

Lahav, O., & Mioduser, D. (2004). Exploration of Unknown Spaces by People Who Are Blind Using a Multi-sensory Virtual Environment. *Journal of Special Education Technology, 19*(3), 15.

Lainema, T. (2009). Perspective Making: Constructivism as a Meaning-Making Structure for Simulation Gaming. *Simulation Gaming, 40*(1), 48-67.

Lawrence, S., & Karen, B. (2009). The rise in autism and the mercury myth. *Journal of Child and Adolescent Psychiatric Nursing, 22*(1), 51-53.

Lawson, J., Baron-Cohen, S., & Wheelwright, S. (2004). Empathising and systemizing in adults with and without Asperger syndrome. *Journal of Autism and Developmental Disorders, 34*(3), 301-310.

Lebeer, J. (2008). Cognitive modifiability, neuroplasticity, and ecology. In Tan, O. S., & Seng, S.H.A. (Eds). *Cognitive modifiability in learning and assessment : international perspectives*. (pp. 83-110). Singapore: Cengage Learning.

Lewis-Beck, M. S., Bryman, A., & Liao, T. F. (2004). *The Sage encyclopaedia of social science research methods*. London, UK: SAGE.

Lipschultz, D. (2009). Gaming @ your library. (Cover story). *American Libraries, 40*(1/2), 40-43.

Martin, A. V., & Christopher, L. (2008). Autism: A review of biological bases, assessment, and intervention. *School Psychology Quarterly, 23*(2), 258-270.

Maslow, A. H. (1968). *Toward a psychology of being* (2nd ed.). Princeton, N.J.: Van Nostrand

Mayo, M. J. (2009). Video Games: A Route to Large-Scale STEM Education? *Science, 323*(5910), 79-82.

Mentis, M., Dunn-Bernstein, M. & Mentis, M. (2008). *Mediated Learning: Teaching, Tasks, and Tools to Unlock Cognitive Potential* (2nd ed.). Thousand Oaks, CA: Corwin Press

Mitchell, P., Parsons, S., & Leonard, A. (2007). Using Virtual Environments for Teaching Social Understanding to 6 Adolescents with Autistic Spectrum Disorders. *Journal of Autism and Developmental Disorders, 37*(3), 589.

Moore, D., Cheng, Y., McGrath, P., & Powell, N., J. (2005). Collaborative Virtual Environment Technology for People With Autism. *Focus on Autism and Other Developmental Disabilities, 20*(4), 231.

Mootz, F. J., III. (2007). Responding to Nietzsche: The Constructive Power of Destruktion. *Law, Culture and the Humanities, 3*(1), 127-154.

Moreno-Ger, P., Burgos, D., & Torrente, J. (2009). Digital Games in eLearning Environments: Current Uses and Emerging Trends. *Simulation Gaming, 40*(5), 669-687.

Parsons, S., Mitchell, P., & Leonard, A. (2004). The Use and Understanding of Virtual Environments by Adolescents with Autistic Spectrum Disorders. *Journal of Autism & Developmental Disorders, 34*(4), 449-466.

Peshkin, A. (1988). In Search of Subjectivity-One's Own. *Educational Researcher, 17*(7), 17-21.

Polkinghorne, D. E. (1995). Narrative configuration in qualitative analysis. International *Journal of Qualitative Studies in Education, 8*(1), 5-23.

Poon, K. (Ed.) (2009). *Educating students with autism spectrum disorders: Making schools meaningful.* Singapore: Prentice Hall.

Prensky, M. (2006). *"Don't bother me Mom, I'm learning!" : How computer and video games are preparing your kids for twenty-first century success and how you can help!.* US: Paragon House.

Prensky, M. (2007). *Digital game-based learning*. US: Paragon House.

Reid, D., & Campbell, K. (2006). The Use of Virtual Reality with Children with Cerebral Palsy: A Pilot Randomized Trial. *Therapeutic Recreation Journal, 40*(4), 255-268.

Rogoff, B. (1990). *Apprenticeship in thinking: Cognitive development in social context*. New York, NY: Oxford University Press.

Rogoff, B. (1993). Children's Guided participatory Appropriation in Sociocultural Activity. In Wozniak, R. H., & Fischer, K. W. (Eds). *Development in context: Acting and thinking in specific environments*. Hillsdale, NJ: Lawrence Erlbaum

Rosas, R., Nussbaum, M., Cumsille, P., Marianov, V., Correa, M.,Flores, P., et al., (2003). Beyond Nintendo: design and assessment of educational video games for first and second grade students. *Computers and Education, 40*, 71-94.

Scahil, L., & Bearss, K. (2009). The rise in autism and the mercury myth. *Journal of Child and Adolescent Psychiatric Nursing, 22*(1), 51-53.

Schank, R. C. (2002). *Designing World-Class E-Learning.* US: McGraw-Hill.

Seng, A. S. H., Pou, L. K. H., & Tan, O. S. (Eds.). (2003). *Mediated learning experience with children : applications across contexts*. Singapore: McGraw-Hill Education (Asia).

Shaffer, D. W. (2006). *How computer games help children learn*. New York, NY: Palgrave Macmillan

Shing, Y.L, Brehmer, Y., & Li, S.C. (2008). Cognitive Plasticity and Training across the Lifespan. In Tan, O. S., & Seng, S.H.A. (Eds.). (2008). *Cognitive modifiability in learning and assessment : international perspectives*. Singapore: Cengage Learning.

Siegel, B. (2003). *Helping children with autism learn treatment approaches for parents and professionals*. New York, NY: Oxford University Press.

Simpson, E., S. (2005). Evolution in the Classroom: What Teachers Need to Know about the Video Game Generation. *TechTrends, 49*(5), 17.

Squire, K. D. (2008). Video Game-Based Learning: An Emerging Paradigm for Instruction. *Performance Improvement Quarterly, 21*(2), 7-36.

Sreedharan, S., Zurita, E. S., & Plimmer, B. (2007). 3D input for 3D worlds. Paper presented at the *OzCHI 2007 Proceedings*, Australia. 227-230. *http://portal.acm.org/citation.cfm?doid=1324892.1324940*

Tan, O. S., & Seng, S.H.A. (Eds.). (2008). *Cognitive modifiability in learning and assessment : international perspectives*. Singapore: Cengage Learning.

Wakabayashi, A., Baron-Cohen, S., Uchiyama, T., Yoshida, Y., Kuroda, M., & Wheelwright, S. (2007). Empathizing and systemizing in adults with and without autism spectrum conditions: Cross-cultural stability. *Journal of Autism and Developmental Disorders*, *37*(10), 1823.

Webb, J., Schirato, T., & Danaher. G. (2002). *Understanding Bourdieu.* Sage.

Wideman, H. H., Owston, R. D., Brown, C., Kushniruk, A., Ho, F., & Pitts, K. C. (2007). Unpacking the potential of educational gaming: A new tool for gaming research. *Simulation & Gaming*, *38*(1), 10-30. doi:10.1177/1046878106297650

Wilson, B. G. & Myres, K. M. (2000). Situated cognition in theoretical and practical context. In *Theoretical Foundations of Learning Environments*. US: Lawrence Erlbaum Associates.

Wilson, K. A., Bedwell, W. L., Lazzara, E. H., Salas, E., Burke, C. S., Estock, J. L., et al. (2009). Relationships Between Game Attributes and Learning Outcomes: Review and Research Proposals. *Simulation Gaming, 40*(2), 217-266. doi:10.1177/1046878108321866

In: Interactive and Digital Media for Education in Virtual … ISBN: 978-1-61668-844-8
Editor: Cai Yiyu

Chapter 8

THE VR CLASSROOM @ RIVER VALLEY HIGH SCHOOL

Ban Hoe Chow and Kah Lay So
River Valley High School, Republic of Singapore

ABSTRACT

Virtual reality (VR) is a revolutionary technology which features reality constructed in a computer-generated artificial world. To date, it has many practical uses in gaming, entertainment and medical applications. VR offers a next-generation teaching tool for in-depth and interactive learning using 3D Immersive Technology.

In July 2007, River Valley High School (RVHS) brings VR into education with the establishment of our very own VR Classroom. Its teaching resources are designed by teachers with a clear objective in mind – to bring learning to another dimension, enabling students to visualise and construct a better understanding of complex worlds from biomolecules, cell structure, to human anatomy. This would help students to gain a deeper and better understanding of difficult concepts in Biology. The VR Classroom does not involve teachers alone. Students are also part of this exciting journey as they take part in student-based project work on 3D immersive technology.

Keywords: Virtual Reality; 3D immersive learning; Life Science

INTRODUCTION

3D is not new. In the 1960s, Ivan Sutherland invented the world's first virtual reality (VR) device, a head-mounted display unit (Sutherland, 1968). In the article "The Ultimate Display", he also described: "the screen is a window through which one sees a virtual world. The challenge is to make that world look real, sound real, act real and feel real (Sutherland, 1970)". To date, VR can be seen in many applications (Kalawsky, 1993; Burdea & Coiffet, 1994). In the defence science, VR is used in fighter plane simulation. In the automobile industry, VR is used for new car design and prototyping. VR is also widely used for diagnosis and pre-treatment planning of neurological surgery. In addition, in the entertainment business, VR provides tourists an immersive experience of flying virtually across geographical sites like the Grand Canyon.

One form of VR representations involves the projection of highly realistic images projected onto large anti-reflection screens with the aid of high performance graphic computing systems to generate the visual and dynamic impact. The high cost for setting up VR infrastructures, however, has limited its applications to only major research and industrial organisations, or institutions of high learning. To our knowledge, no secondary school in the world was reported before 2007 to be equipped with a 3D immersive VR facility for learning purposes. Recent advances in graphics display hardware and computing technology has made it possible to offer affordable, yet as effective VR solutions for classroom teaching and learning in schools.

This chapter reports our experience of using 3D immersive VR for curriculum-based classroom teaching and co-curricular student-centred activities. It describes the VR Classroom set up in RVHS and discusses the curriculum design in the VR Classroom, as well as related interesting student-based project work.

THE VR CLASSROOM

Our VR Classroom (Figure 1) is constructed with high-end graphics and display hardware, and high performance computing technology. The system supports real-time, realistic visualisation and modelling in the classroom teaching within the facility.

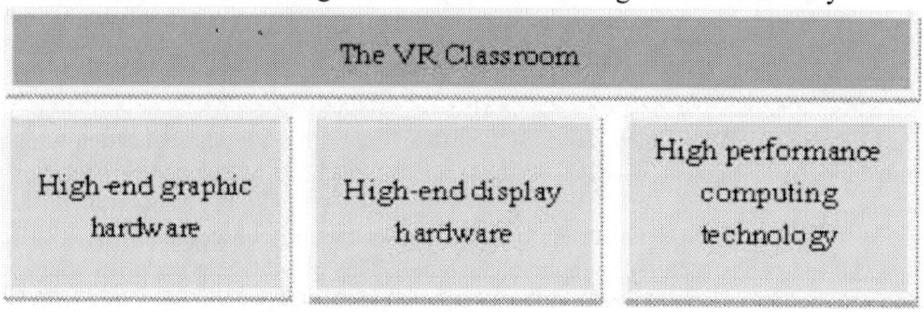

Figure 1. Graphics, display and computing technology for the VR Classroom.

THE INFRASTRUCTURE DESIGN OF THE VR CLASSROOM

The design of the VR Classroom takes into account various factors in classroom teaching. An existing room in our school is selected as a physical site for the VR Classroom (Figure 2). Basic renovation is carried out in the classroom to cater to a standard class of about 30 students. A front projection system is adopted due to the room dimensions and the provision of a free seating space within a suitable field of view (FOV). High quality immersive effects are generated from the integration of the high quality images projected on an anti-reflective screen.

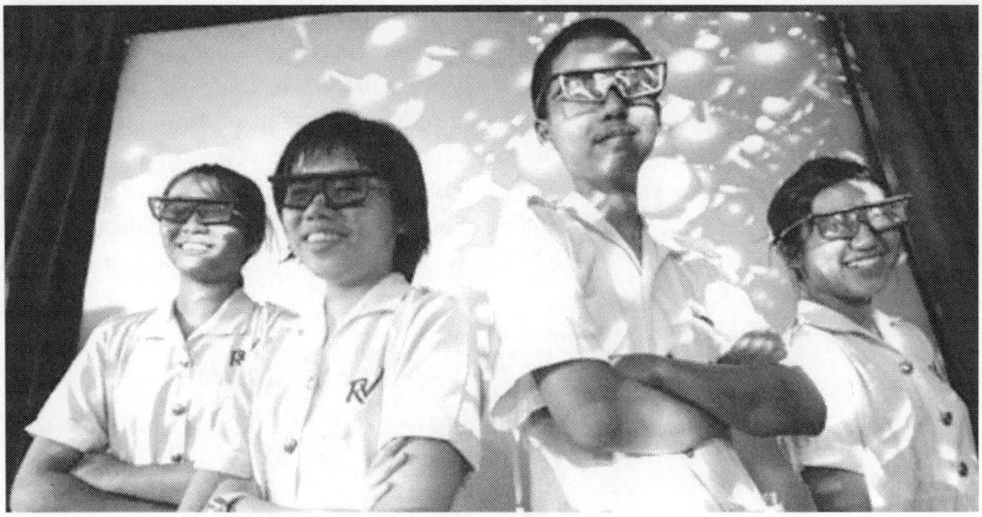

Figure 2. The VR Classroom @ RVHS.

The Curriculum Contents of the VR Classroom

The curriculum contents of the VR classroom are designed with infusion of 3D immersive technology. The 3D immersive environment enables students to reach many complex and dynamic worlds to aid in their learning. With immersive visualisation, students can gain a deeper and better understanding of difficult concepts in virtual worlds, where size really does not matter (Table 1). The topics in the VR Classroom can cover objects ranging from very tiny structures, such as DNA biomolecules to large entities like the solar system, as well as their related processes and phenomena.

Table 1. Sample Content Design

Topic	Size	Process
DNA	2.3 nm	Replication
Protein	15 nm	Transcription & translation
Cell	1 nm	Cell division
Virus	1 μm	Host cell infection
Human anatomy and physiology	Visible to naked eye	Digestion
Solar system	Light years	Revolution of planets

Visual based learning or visual learning is a primary style of cognitive learning. Visual learning involves the association of ideas, concepts and data with visual information, which includes images and models. Visual learning pedagogy helps to enhance learning, recognition and retention of information by representing information spatially with images and models. It helps learners to better focus on learning and grouping similar ideas easily, as well as, allowing better organisation of learners' visual cognitive load.

Visual learning environments, especially in an immersive learning environment may help in engaging the learners and motivating their learning interests. It also facilitates learners' critical thinking, retention, comprehension and organisation. The teaching resources designed for the VR Classroom takes advantage of 3D visual learning. Some concepts that students have difficulty in understanding can be taught and learnt more effectively with the aid of 3D visualisation. Various 3D resources are developed to assist students' learning, especially of complicated microscopic structures and dynamic processes in selected topics in Biology. Students put on 3D glasses to view 3D immersive animation movies and posters, and this teleports them into a dynamic, colourful and fascinating world of cells and molecules, hence making Biology come alive for our learners. Figure 3 shows the teaching and learning of the structure of DNA in the VR Classroom.

Figure 3. Learning and teaching in the VR Classroom.

By associating with 3D visual information in the VR Classroom, students can better understand and assimilate concepts more effectively. They also connect and relate better to visually represented information, especially with complex ideas. In addition, representation of academic contents as 3D dynamic visualisations can further aid students in the recall of concepts

CURRICULUM-BASED TEACHING IN THE VR CLASSROOM

The Framework of Teaching for Understanding

The learning of concepts in Biology can be enhanced with the VR Classroom. 3D Immersive Technology provides direct support for the framework of "Teaching for Understanding", where the emphasis on curriculum design is to develop and enhance students' understanding, as described in this sample lesson outline. The VR Classroom can help engage students as they actively participate in the lesson. Here the 3D learning environment is designed not only to support students' construction of knowledge in a meaningful way but also to help them be responsible for their own learning.

A Sample Lesson Outline

Subject	Biology
Unit	Continuity of Life
Level	Year 3 (age: 15)
Duration	60 minutes
Topic	DNA Structure & Function
Understanding Goals	Students will appreciate the molecular structure of DNA double helix and understand how it determines life.
Background Knowledge	Students should have a good understanding of: • ultrastructure of cells, and • chemical bonding and structure in Chemistry
Main VR Materials	3-D movie "The Virtual Cell" 3-D molecular animations 3-D posters of animal / plant cell & DNA structure Anaglyph and polarising glasses
Complementary Material	Molymod™ molecular model of DNA Skeletal model of DNA Poster of Watson, Crick & DNA Student handouts
Interactive instruction	Illustrate molecular structures of different components of DNA. Rotate molecules to different orientations to help students visualise 3-D stereoscopic views of various parts of DNA and RNA: • pentose sugar (deoxyribose vs ribose) • nitrogenous bases (adenine, thymine, guanine, cytosine and uracil) • sugar-phosphate backbone • double-stranded DNA

This VR learning environment enables students to build upon their capacity for learning, energises students to learn, and can even involve the collaboration with other learners. The teaching resources developed took various forms of media, from animation video clips or movies, 3D molecular models to anaglyph posters and wall papers (Figure 4).

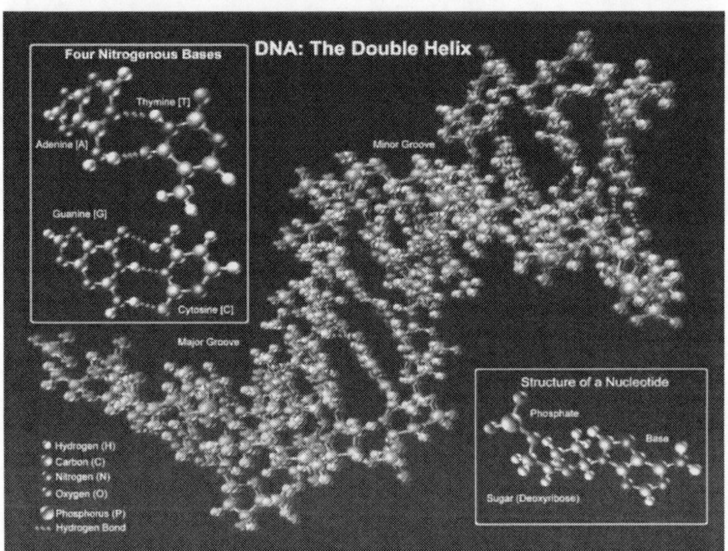

Figure 4. The 3D anaglyph poster of DNA.

Experience the 3D Immersive and Interactive Technology

Figure 5. Student identifying components of a DNA molecule.

Figure 5 shows a student identifying various components (e.g. sugar and phosphate group) on the 3D screen. Through hands-on activities, students demonstrate their perception and understanding in the recognition of parts of the DNA molecular structure in different 3D spatial orientation.

The teacher uses Socratic questioning to guide students in deducing and reasoning out the structure of DNA the way the DNA model is unravelled by biochemists. They will relate the design of DNA structure better in relation to its function, as well as, how the genetic code is stored in DNA.

As seen with this Biology example, the beauty of 3D immersive technology is not only that it stands out as visually and dynamically engaging for our learners, it also can be easily adapted for any subject with abstract contents, e.g. 3-D solids and angles in Mathematics, stereoisomerism of organic molecules in Chemistry.

Students' Feedback

The results of a post-lesson survey showed favourable feedback from our students on the learning in the VR Classroom. The responses to three general questions posed are as follows:

1) Which part of the 3D aspects of the lesson do you like best? You can choose more than one.

   - Animation [32, 96.9%]
   - DNA software [9, 27.3%]
   - Poster [0, 0.0%]

2) Has this lesson in the VR Classroom helped you in the understanding the subject better? Regardless if you had a little or no prior knowledge of the subject just taught.

   - Yes [32, 96.9%]
   - No [1, 3.0%]

3) Did today's lesson in the VR classroom help you generate more interest in the subject/topic that was taught?

   - Yes [30, 90.9%]
   - No [3, 9.1%]

Comments from students also indicated that they welcomed and appreciated this innovative teaching strategy:

1) I feel invigorated and enthused by the 3D animated cells and it's indeed a very fulfilling experience for me. Now, I think I would like the Biology lessons more than ever as we dive deeper into the world of human biological cells. I would like other schools to have such special lessons too.

   – Jadeline

2) It's fun to see the 3D cells rather than 2D ones in photographs. The video has enhanced my understanding of cells and the lesson is engaging. Now I am keen to learn more and I hope there will be animation for other biology topics.

   – Madeline

3) The 3D animation has really helped me gain another outlook in the structure and internal working of cells, plus illustrate effectively the units of DNA, which was very interesting, and as good, if not better than a practical lesson.

   – Jian Qin

Co-Curricular Student-Centred Activities in the VR Classroom

The VR Classroom is not just a collaborative project between the teachers and external partners. With the establishment of the VR Classroom in RVHS, besides the academic curriculum, the facility has also spun off a multitude of student-based projects. These involvements allow students to partake and learn through this joint venture in the use of virtual reality.

Bilingual Media Creation

River Valley High School is a government school under the Special Assistance Plan scheme, which promotes the mission in the inculcation of Chinese and Chinese culture at an extensive level. Our students are effectively bilingual and a project team took the lead in translating the teaching resources, such as the movie narration and captions on 3D posters into Chinese in 2008, hence providing an alternative medium of instruction for a bilingual school like ours.

Nanyang Research Programme

From 2007 to 2010, groups of students work on research projects on the design of 3D interactive media under the mentorship of Associate Professor Cai Yiyu, of the School of Mechanical and Aerospace Engineering, Nanyang Technological University, as part of the Nanyang Research Programme (NRP). The students' work won Gold Awards for three consecutive years in the annual NRP Symposium in 2008, 2009 and 2010.

Use of Mixed Reality in Education of School History

Founded in 1956, River Valley High School was the first Chinese secondary school set up by the Singapore government. Initially known as the Singapore Government Chinese Middle School at the current premises of Seng Poh Primary School, it was renamed to Queenstown Government Chinese Middle School when moved to Strathmore Avenue. In 1958, it was relocated to Jalan Kuala and renamed River Valley Government Chinese Middle School. The school then moved to West Coast Road in 1986. It then moved once again to a holding site at Malan Road in 2006. The school finally relocates to Boon Lay Avenue in 2010.

Throughout the 53 years of RVHS history, there have been several memorial campus shifts. For each and every campus, history is rewritten. An NRP project team formed by RVHS students makes use of mixed reality (MR) technology to model and construct virtually the buildings at these campuses of the past, the present and the future. They also used 3D photography to capture their glimpses of the existing campuses. Combining the 3D models and 3D pictures, this project created MR documentation of the rich school history at the different campuses.

"MR Campuses of RVHS" is a project using the 3D animation and 3D photography technologies for public education on the school history (Figure 6). The project team worked on this project in 2008 to create virtual campuses linking RVHS' 53 years of history through time. The project not only can help other students to better understand the school history, but also can be potentially used for the archival documentation of RVHS' past, present and future.

Figure 6. Mixed Reality campus of RVHS.

Use of Mixed Reality in Education of School Safety and Security

Funded by the Security Awareness for Everyone (SAFE) Programme by the Ministry of Home Affairs, the "MR Campuses of RVHS" project was further extended to generate public awareness of school safety and security in 2009. The completed product, which was a 3D animation movie to introduce safety and security features in the virtual RVHS campus, won the only Gold Award in the Secondary Student Category in the Ministry of Home Affairs Innovation Fest in 2009. The project was again showcased in the Home Team Convention in 2010.

Competitions in Infocommunication Technology

In 2009, the "MR Campuses of RVHS" project also won a Merit Award at the Singapore Infocomm Technology Federation (SiTF) Awards Competition. The SiTF Awards is a local industrial award which recognises the most innovative infocomm technology solutions developed by companies and schools in Singapore. With this success, RVHS proceeded on to the international arena, as one of the two schools to represent Singapore to vie in the prestigious and keenly-contested Asia-Pacific Infocomm Technology Awards (APICTA) Competition held in Melbourne, Australia in December 2009.

Figure 7. RVHS students at MHA Safety and Security Competition.

Conclusion

Visualisation is the representation of a design, concept or idea in a stimulating and realistic manner. Accurately capturing and presenting objects in a 3D form presents a simulated, virtual but realistic learning environment. 3D teaching resources have been proven to be highly effective in promoting students' comprehension of complicated ideas and concepts in River Valley High School's very own Virtual Reality Classroom. In short, this VR Classroom presents a next generation education facility offering infinite possibilities to engage learners and connect them between the borderless real and virtual worlds.

The VR Classroom @ RVHS received the Ministry of Education (MOE) Innergy Silver Award in 2008. The Innergy Award recognises individuals and teams from schools whose innovative ideas have been successfully implemented and contribute significantly to MOE's mission.

Acknowledgments

This project is partially supported by Singapore's Ministry of Education under the LEAD@ICT scheme. The VR Classroom is established by River Valley High School, in collaboration with ZEPTH Pte Ltd.

AUTHORS INFO

Chow Ban Hoe is a high school Biology teacher, while So Kah Lay is the Vice Principal of River Valley High School. The project is supported by the LEAD@ICT scheme of the Ministry of Education, Singapore. This scheme supports the school to achieve a higher level of ICT usage in classrooms and to facilitate the push to more innovative use of ICT in teaching and learning.

CHOW Ban Hoe
River Valley High School, Singapore
Email: chow_ban_hoe@moe.edu.sg

SO Kah Lay
River Valley High School, Singapore
Email: so_kah_lay@moe.gov.sg

REFERENCES

Burdea, G. and Coiffet, P. (1994), Virtual Reality Technology, John Wiley.

Kalawsky, R. S. (1993), The Science of Virtual Reality and Virtual Environments, Addison-Wesley.

Sutherland, I. E. (1968). A head-mounted three dimensional display. In Proceedings of 1968 Fall Joint Computer Conference, pp. 757-764.

Sutherland, I. E. (1970), The Ultimate Display, Scientific American, Vol. 222, No. 6, June, pp. 57-81.

In: Interactive and Digital Media for Education in Virtual … ISBN: 978-1-61668-844-8
Editor: Cai Yiyu

Chapter 9

THE VR ELEMENTS OF GEOMETRY

Gwee Hwee Ngee
Hwa Chong Institution, Republic of Singapore

ABSTRACT

Geometry has a long history. The study of Geometry was part of the culture in Ancient Greece. Euclid wrote *The Elements* in about 300 BC, summarising the work of Greek mathematicians like Pythagoras, Hippocrates, and Theaetetus. It consists of 13 books covering topics from Plane Geometry to Three-dimensional Geometry. Today, Geometry taught in schools very much follows Euclid's ideas.

As an enabling technology, Virtual Reality (VR) has found many applications in Entertainment, Medicine, and Defense Sciences. This chapter addresses a novel application of VR for Geometry Learning. We will first introduce the VR Elements highlighting the major functions and features. A teaching plan on using the VR Elements for Geometry Learning will then be discussed. This will be followed by an initial trial with a small group of students. The student feedback will be discussed.

Keywords: Elements; 3D immersive learning; Interactive learning; Geometry learning

INTRODUCTION

Euclid's *Elements* (Heath 1926) has been a default principal textbook for Geometry learning. It consists of thirteen books: Books 1 - 4 dealing with plane geometry; Books 5 - 10 introducing ratios and proportions; and Books 11 – 13 studying spatial geometry. Typically, high school geometry courses cover several topics following Euclid's *Elements* (Todhunter 1862; Birkhoff 1932; Hartshorne 2000). Todhunter (1862) wrote in the preface of his book: "In England the textbook of Geometry consists of the Elements of Euclid." Birkhoff (1932) advocated the teaching of Geometry based on measurement of distances and angles using real numbers. However, Geometry is taught mainly as a collection of truths (Hartshorne 2000). Geometry is different from other math courses and therefore different thinking skills are needed for Geometry learning and teaching.

Geometry is abstract. It is about critical thinking, learning concepts and principles and knowing when and how to apply them. Usually, plane geometry is relatively simple to students and they are able to understand the properties of planar geometry, for example, angles between two parallel lines illustrated on the traditional blackboard. However, it is not that easy for them to fully understand some concepts of spatial geometry. Often, teachers use a cube model to teach the students that the diagonal lines of two opposite faces are skew. But, it is impossible to show the angle between two skew lines. Thus, students would have to visualise and imagine these difficult concepts by themselves.

As an enabling technology, Virtual Reality (VR) has found many applications in Engineering, Medicine and Entertainment. Also, VR technology has been used for educational purposes (Schmalstieg; Zimmermann, Cunningham *et al.* 1991; Arcavi 2003) focusing on the visualisation of geometrical concepts. Our interest is to develop new VR technology to support students in the learning of Geometry using a more intuitive fashion both visually and interactively.

VR Elements

VR Technology

The VR Elements solution contains both hardware and software components. The hardware component consists of a stereographic sub-system and an interactive sub-system (Fig. 1). The interactive sub-system has 1) a control pad to input system commands and numerical numbers; and 2) a 3D pen to create, edit and manipulate the 3D elements. It has 6 Degree-of-Freedom (6DOF) tracking and 3D digitizing. The 3D pen is used as an input tool which allows various modes, for e.g. insertion, selection, and transformation. In insertion mode, basic Geometry elements can be created. In selection mode, one Geometry element can be selected for modification purpose. If the selection contains two elements, the relationship between the two elements can be derived. In transformation mode, objects can be rotated, translated or scaled with a scene. Fig. 1 shows a user with the control pad and the 3D pen in front of the 3D screen to play with various functions of the VR Elements.

Figure 1. The hardware and software for VR enhanced Geometry learning.

The software part consists of two layers: the core layer and the application layer. The core layer is for the system users to develop the application. In this case, the application layer is basically designed in a user-interface for the learning of fundamental Geometry topics in both 2D and 3D space. The basic Geometry elements of the VR Element are points, lines, planes, cubes, spheres, etc. The properties of each element are listed in Table 1. The relationship between two elements can be obtained with the VR Elements.

Table 1. Properties of Geometry elements

Elements	Properties		
Point	Position	Point thickness	Point color
Line	2 end points	Line thickness	Line color
Plane	3 locations	Four sides	Plane color
Cube	Center	Width, height and depth	Cube color
Sphere	Center	Radius	Sphere Color

Distance

In VR Elements, the distance of any two elements can be measured with the 3D pen. As shown in Fig. 2, point-point distance, point-line distance and point-plane distance can be directly measured interactively. Fig. 2(d-f) shows line-line distance, line-plane distance, and plane-plane distance. The distance between two skew lines (or two parallel lines) can be calculated as well.

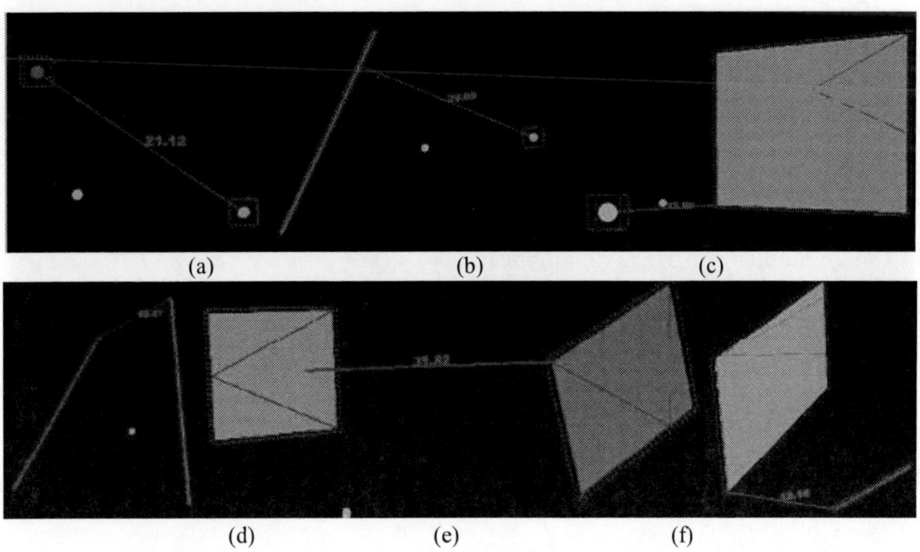

Figure 2. The distance between two elements can be measured in the VR Elements: (a) point-point distance; (b) point-line distance; (c) point-plane distance; (d) line-line distance; (e) plane-plane distance; and (f) line-plane distance.

Angle

In 3D space, two lines may or may not intersect. A line can either intersect with a plane or parallel to a plane. For two planes, they always intersect. VR Elements can measure the angle formed by two intersecting geometric elements. Similar to the measurement of distance, angles can be measured by using the 3D pen in an interactive fashion.

Dynamics

The VR Elements has a dynamic feature which allows the users to dynamically transform any geometric entities. For example, a line segment when selected can be rotated in 3D space. While being rotated in 3D, its associated distance or angle will be dynamically updated.

USING VR ELEMENTS IN CLASSROOM TEACHING

The VR Elements will be used and fit in with the requirements of the Singapore Mathematics syllabi, on the topic of three-dimensional Trigonometry. In this topic, teachers would need to cover the concepts of angles between lines and planes in 3D along with the trigonometric calculations. As mentioned previously, this topic is most difficult to be taught using the traditional blackboard thus it has been selected for this teaching plan.

Lesson Objectives

At the end of the lesson, students should be able to

[1] calculate angles between two planes
[2] calculate angles between a straight line and a plane
[3] solve problems in 3D involving angles of elevation and depression
[4] solve problems in 3D involving bearings

Lesson Aims

[1] Introduce VR Elements as a tool for classroom teaching and learning
[2] Using VR Elements to support the learning of Geometry through a visual and interactive manner

Teaching Plan

Time	Plan	Remarks	Materials
10 mins	Introduction	Generate students' Interest by finding out their personal experience on Virtual Reality for e.g. Omni-Max Shows, 3D movies Teacher to show some real life products created using the VR Elements	
15 mins	Demonstration	Teacher to demonstrate the use of VR Elements with aid of 3D pen * Line – Plane Relationship * Plane – Plane Relationship * Rotation of Plane or Points to emphasize that Seeing is NOT Believing! * Measurement of Distances and Angles	Virtual Lab Examples using VR Elements
10 mins	Student Participation	Some students invited to try out using the VR technology	
10 mins	Teacher Demonstration	Teacher to use some examples from powerpoint slides and worksheets to show students how to calculate angles between two planes or straight line and plane	Powerpoint slides and Wor-ksheets
10 mins	Problem Sovling	Students to solve problems on worksheet involving angle calculation and bearings	Worksheet
5 mins	Lesson Closure	Teacher to gather feedback from students	

STUDENTS' INITIAL TRIAL

The initial trial of VR Elements was carried out on 17th November in the VR Lab at Hwa Chong Institution, involving 5 Secondary 2 students, aged between 13 – 14 years old.

The purpose of the trial was explained to the students, followed by a demonstration of the VR Elements. The students were shown a cube which can be rotated using the 3D pen, angles and distances were correspondingly measured. Each of the students was then given the opportunity to try out the VR technology.

Student A tried to use the pen to draw a triangle on the VR screen. However, when it was rotated, he realized that that the vertices of the triangle did not meet on the same plane!

Student B tried to use the pen to draw an additional line to the original cube and measured the corresponding angles and distances.

Most of the students were positive about the experience of using the VR technology and felt that it was a suitable addition to the Math curriculum. They were keen to find out when they would be learning the concepts in the coming year! Some of them were also curious to find out how the technology worked and this opportunity gave them a chance to think about 2D and 3D visualization. There were others, on the other hand, who were interested to know how they can make use of the technology in 3D designing.

Some students, however, were uncomfortable with the use of the pen and glasses. Being their first time using such technology, they felt the pen was too sensitive and difficult to control and the glasses were flimsy and they were a little giddy at the end of the session.

Figure 3. Students interact with the geometric objects in 3D.

Conclusion

This chapter discusses the application of VR technology for Geometry learning. Following Euclid's idea of The Elements of Geometry, the proposed research has a focus on the use of a 3D interactive solution for learning fundamental topics or concepts in Geometry.

Acknowledgments

The VR Elements is developed by ZEPTH Pte Ltd.

Authors Info

Gwee Hwee Ngee is a mathematics teacher with Hwa Chong Institution, Singapore. This project is supported by National Research Foundation, Singapore.

Gwee Hwee Ngee
Hwa Chong Institution
Republic of Singapore
Email: gweehn@hci.edu.sg

References

Arcavi, A. (2003). "The role of visual representations in the learning of mathematics." *Educational Studies in Mathematics* 52(3): 215-241.

Birkhoff, G. D. (1932). "A set of postulates for plane Geometry, based on scale and protractor." *Annals of Mathematics*: 329-345.

Hartshorne, R. (2000). "Teaching Geometry According to Euclid." *NOTICES-AMERICAN MATHEMATICAL SOCIETY* 47(4): 460-465.

Heath, T. (1926). *The thirteen books of Euclid's Elements. Translated from the text of Heiberg with introduction and commentary*, Cambridge: University Press.

Schmalstieg D. "Designing immersive virtual reality for Geometry education." *IEEE Virtual Reality*, Alexandria, VA, USA, March_27.

Todhunter, I. (1862). *The Elements of Euclid for the Use of Schools and Colleges*, Macmillan.

Zimmermann, W., S. Cunningham, *et al.* (1991). *Visualization in teaching and learning mathematics*, Mathematical Association of America Washington, DC, USA.

INDEX

D

E

F

G

H

Q

R

S

T

U

V

W

Y